E-Collar Training Step-by-Step

A How-To Innovative Guide to Positively Train Your Dog through E-collars; Tips and Tricks and Effective Techniques for Different Species of Dogs

Paul Davis

© Copyright 2019 - All rights reserved.

The content contained within this book may not be reproduced, duplicated or transmitted without direct written permission from the author or the publisher.

Under no circumstances will any blame or legal responsibility be held against the publisher, or author, for any damages, reparation, or monetary loss due to the information contained within this book, either directly or indirectly.

Legal Notice:

This book is copyright protected. It is only for personal use. You cannot amend, distribute, sell, use, quote or paraphrase any part, or the content within this book, without the consent of the author or publisher.

Disclaimer Notice:

Please note the information contained within this document is for educational and entertainment purposes only. All effort has been executed to present accurate, up to date, reliable, complete information. No warranties of any kind are declared or implied. Readers acknowledge that the author is not engaging in the rendering of legal, financial, medical or professional advice. The content within this book has been derived from various sources. Please consult a licensed professional before attempting any techniques outlined in this book.

By reading this document, the reader agrees that under no circumstances is the author responsible for any losses, direct or indirect, that are incurred as a result of the use of information contained within this document, including, but not limited to, errors, omissions, or inaccuracies.

Table of Contents

Introduction 1

CHAPTER 1
CHOOSING THE RIGHT DOG FOR YOU 4

TIPS FOR CHOOSING THE BEST DOG FOR YOU 4
    Dogs Are Not Cheap 4
    Plan for Your Dog's Arrival 5
    You Need to Exercise Your Dog 6
    Most Dogs Live for 10 Years or More 6
    Most Dogs Require Grooming 7
    A Puppy Doesn't Stay Small Forever 7
    Can You Meet the Parents? 8
CHOOSING THE BEST BREED FOR TRAINING 8
    What Makes a Dog Easily Trainable? 8
    Best Breeds for Training 9
WHERE TO GO? 14
    Adoption 14
    Pet Store 16
    Responsible Breeders 16
    Social Media 16
TIPS TO KEEP IN MIND BEFORE BRINGING YOUR DOG HOME 17

CHAPTER 2
E-COLLAR BASICS 20

WHAT IS THE E-COLLAR? 21
TYPES OF E-COLLARS 22
    Yard Training 22
    Hunting Training 23
    Work Training 23
    No-Bark E-Collar 24
E-COLLAR ACCESSORIES 25
HOW TO USE AN E-COLLAR 26
    Parts and Terminology 26
    Step One: Read the Instructions 27
    Step Two: Place the Batteries Into the Transmitter 27
    Step Three: Fit the E-Collar on Your Dog's Neck 27
    Step Four: Let Your Dog Adjust to the E-Collar for a Week 28
    Step Five: Start Using the E-Collar 28
    Step Six: Start with Commands Your Dog Understands 29
    Step Seven: Control Your Dog's Negative Behavior 29

- E-COLLAR SAFETY 30
  - Don't Leave Your Dog Unattended with an E-Collar 30
  - Understand Your E-Collar 30
  - Don't Use a Leash with the E-Collar 30
  - Don't Use the E-Collar When Your Dog is Swimming 31
- BENEFITS OF AN E-COLLAR 31
  - Fast Results 31
  - Long Lasting Behavioral Changes 32
  - E-Collars Don't Take a Lot of Strength 32
  - You Don't Stress Your Voice 32
  - E-Collars Allow for Easier Consistency 33
  - Your Dog Receives Off-Leash Freedom 33
- COMMON MYTHS ABOUT THE E-COLLAR 34
  - The Shocks Harm Your Dog 34
  - Only Professional Trainers Can Use E-collars 34
  - The E-Collar Burns Your Dog 35
  - The E-Collar Leaves Marks On the Dog's Neck 35

CHAPTER 3
YOUR DOG AND THEIR E-COLLAR 36

- CHOOSING THE BEST E-COLLAR 36
  - The Fundamental Five 36
- YOUR DOG'S REACTION TO THE E-COLLAR 38
  - Unintended Reactions 38
  - What If Your Dog Is Scared of the E-Collar 40
  - The Story of Frankie and her E-Collar 42

CHAPTER 4
WHAT YOU NEED TO KNOW BEFORE TRAINING BEGINS 44

- GENERAL TRAINING TIPS FOR DOGS AT ANY AGE 44
  - Know Your House Rules 45
  - Always Be Consistent 45
  - Stay Healthy 48
  - Be Patient 49
  - Reward Good Behavior 51
  - Obedience Classes 51
  - Your Dog's Age Matters 53
- TRAINING YOUR PUPPY 55
  - Your Puppy is Not an Infant and Not an Adult 55
  - Your Puppy's Developmental Stages 55
  - A Puppy's Fears 57
  - Don't Start House Training Until Eight Weeks Old 58
  - Training a Puppy Takes a Certain Mindset 58
- TRAINING YOUR OLDER DOG 58
  - You Can Train Them for a Longer Period of Time 59
  - You Need More Patience 59

Socialize Your Dog *60*
Get to Know Your Dog *60*

CHAPTER 5
LET THE TRAINING BEGIN 61

TIPS TO PREPARE YOUR DOG FOR TRAINING 61
Always Have Your Dog's Attention Prior to Training *61*
Make Sure You Have a Little Play Time *61*
Have Everything You Need with You *62*
Empty Your Dog's Stomach *62*
Every Dog Should Know the Basic Commands *62*

BASIC COMMANDS 63
Bed Training *63*
Home Base and Perimeter Training *65*
Sit Training *69*
Lay Down Training *71*
Come Training *72*
Stay Training *74*
Get Down Training *75*

CHAPTER 6
TRAINING STRATEGIES, LEVELS, AND YOUR DOG 77

TRAINING LEVELS 77
Level One: Foundation Training *78*
Level Two: Skill Building Training *78*
Level Three: Reinforce Reliability and Behaviors *78*
Level Four: Advanced Skills *79*
Level Five: Expert Training Skills *80*

PRACTICE REAL LIFE TRAINING 81
Practice Sitting Politely *81*
Use "Come" When You Get a Chance *83*
Take Your Dog for Car Rides *84*
Aggressive Dogs *86*

INTERMEDIATE LEVEL TRICKS FOR DOGS 89
Fetch *89*
Spin and Twist *92*

CHAPTER 7
ADVANCED TRAINING WITH E-COLLARS 95

WILL I STOP TRAINING? 95
READJUSTING THE E-COLLAR FOR A GROWING DOG 96
AGILITY TRAINING 96
Basic Training Before the E-Collar *97*
Agility Training Is Great for Your Dog's Health *97*
There Are Risks *97*
Using the E-Collar *98*

    Adding New Skills 98
    Roxie Jumped Over a Bar 99
    Boing 100
  HUNTING 101
    Teach Your Dog the Route 102
    Make Sure to Train Your Dog to Return Home 102
    Repetition Is Key 102

CHAPTER 8
COMMON MISTAKES 103

  LACK OF CONSISTENCY IN TRAINING 103
  TRAINING YOUR DOG FOR TOO LONG 103
  DOG OWNERS DON'T SEND A SIGNAL IMMEDIATELY 104
  YOU WAIT TOO LONG TO START TRAINING 105
  PEOPLE BECOME CODEPENDENT ON THE E-COLLAR 105
  YOU DON'T GIVE YOUR DOG ENOUGH TRAINING TIME 105
  THE DOG HAS NOT RECEIVED ANY TYPE OF PRIOR TRAINING 106
  YOU USE HARSH DISCIPLINE 107
  PEOPLE DON'T UNDERSTAND HOW THE E-COLLAR WORKS 107

CHAPTER 9
FREQUENTLY ASKED QUESTIONS AND ANSWERS 108

  QUESTION #1: DO DIFFERENT BREEDS OF DOGS LEARN DIFFERENTLY? 108
  QUESTIONS #2: DO I WEAN MY DOG OFF THE E-COLLAR? 109
  QUESTION #3: HOW DO I KNOW THE E-COLLAR ISN'T HARMING MY DOG? .. 109
  QUESTION #4: HOW DO I KNOW WHEN TO START USING THE E-COLLAR? 110
  QUESTION #5: I HAVE SEEN OTHER DOGS REACT NEGATIVELY TO THE SHOCK FROM THE E-COLLAR. HOW DO I KNOW MY DOG WON'T? 110

CONCLUSION 112
REFERENCES 117

Introduction

You are at your local animal shelter looking through the cages. You walk by slowly, talking to each dog. "Hey there, how are you doing today?" you say to each one of the dogs as you read the little notecard of information attached to the cage. It's so hard to choose one dog to bring home. You want to bring them all home. But you know that you need to pick the best dog for yourself, your family, and think of the dog.

Living in an apartment, you realize a smaller dog is best. It will get exercise by running around the apartment easier than a larger dog will. You also know you need a dog that is comfortable around kids, won't get lonely easily, and is easily trainable. With you and your husband working full-time jobs, you can't be home all the time for your new pup.

Through your research, you know many breeds of smaller dogs are easily trainable. Walking by a cage, you see a Miniature Schnauzer named Phillip. You smile at Phillip as you read information about him. He is three years old, neutered, enjoys children, and has received basic training. Through your conversation with the shelter employee, you find out that the employees are training Phillip with an e-collar or electronic collar. You know very little about this device, so the employee shows you how it works.

This book is going to take you through everything you need to know about e-collar training and your dog. You will not only learn the basics of e-collar training, but you'll learn how to help your dog thrive. Diving into Chapter 1, you will get basic information, such as easily trainable dog breeds, what factors to think of when you are choosing the best dog for you, how to care for your dog, and where to go to choose your dog.

Chapter 2 will give you information on e-collar basics. After learning what an e-collar is, you can discover the types of e-collars and accessories available for your dog. This chapter will also give you a step-by-step guide on how to use an e-collar. Of course, you can't learn how to use an e-collar without learning about the safety of e-collars. If you are still unsure if e-collar is the way to go, Chapter 2 debunks several myths that people have about e-collars.

Deciding that you want the e-collar, you wonder how it will affect your dog. Is there a certain e-collar you should choose? What will your dog's reaction be? Instead of wondering about these questions, it's time to read Chapter 3. In this chapter, you will learn about the fundamental five when it comes to picking the right e-collar for your dog. You will also read about a couple of case examples when it comes to the unintended consequences of an e-collar your dog can have if you do not train them properly.

Chapter 4 gives you everything you need to know before you begin training. You will receive general tips on training a dog at any age, information on obedience classes, and how your dog's age matters when it comes to training. To give you the greatest amount of information possible so you are prepared to start training your dog, this chapter gives you tips for training your puppy and tips for training an older dog.

Finally, in Chapter 5, you can let the training begin. This chapter starts with giving you tips to prepare your dog for training. You will then get a step by step guide on how to train your dog with the basic commands, such as bed training, home base training, sitting, laying down, and getting down.

Chapter 6 goes a little further into training by looking at the training levels you will reach if you enroll your dog in obedience school. Of course, you can always focus on training your dog through these levels in your home. One of the best parts of this chapter is that it gives you some real life training examples so you know what to do when you are practicing training your dog in a real setting, such as bringing them on a car ride or to a dog-friendly store. You will also receive information on how to handle aggressiveness from dogs and some intermediate level tricks, such as teaching your dog to play fetch.

The advanced training shows up in Chapter 7. Not only is the popular question of "Will I ever stop training my dog" be answered, but you will read tips about agility training and hunting. You can also learn a couple of fun tricks to see if your dog would be great at agility training.

What are the most common mistakes dog owners make and how you can pay attention so you don't make the same mistakes? You can find out all this information in Chapter 8. You will learn how discipline doesn't really help your dog, though most people incorporate time out when their dog does something like scratch up the wall.

This book will round off with Chapter 9, which discusses a number of common questions people have about dog training. Of course, you will get the answers to these questions!

Now that I have given you the rundown for what you are about to learn, it's time to dive into the wonderful information!

Chapter 1:

Choosing the Right Dog for You

Choosing the right dog can be a big decision. While sometimes it seems that the right dog just "falls into your lap," other times you search for days or weeks. There are a lot of factors that influence your decision in getting a dog. For example, if you don't have a lot of money to put toward a dog, you look for a free dog or one from the shelter that is already fixed. If you live in an apartment, you may feel it is easier to get a small dog.

Tips for Choosing the Best Dog for You

With over 200 breeds of dogs, it's impossible to discuss all of them. Instead, I want to focus on tips that will help you choose the best dog for you.

Dogs Are Not Cheap

One factor to consider is how much money you can put toward a dog. While they are cheaper than children, they still need to go to the vet, they need food, toys, a crate, a leash, bowls for their food and water, grooming, and training tools or classes. Just because you got a dog for free from a social media site or your neighbor, does not mean that you will never put money toward your dog. Plus, most people like to spoil their dog with a sweater, especially if they live in colder temperatures.

Plan for Your Dog's Arrival

It is important to not just bring a dog home without any preparation. You want to prepare a place for your dog just like you would any member of your family. Just like humans, animals have feelings. They also need to feel a certain way to grow within their new home.

If you have an older dog, you won't have to worry about "puppy proofing" your home. However, you will still want to ensure that you pick up anything the dog can harm themselves with. Even senior dogs will find interest in a screwdriver or want to taste the chocolate within their reach.

If you are bringing home a puppy, you will want to make sure that you puppy proof your entire home–you will be amazed at what a puppy can get into. For instance, you will want to ensure all your valuables are not in the puppy's reach. Remember, your puppy will be full of energy and into jumping. You will also want to secure any wires because puppies love to chew on anything.

You also need to think about what the dog needs. Some of the factors to think about are:

- *Security.* Just like people, one of the biggest ways to make a dog feel at home is to make them feel safe.

- *Love.* You will need to spend time with your dog and make sure they are adjusting well. They will need a lot of physical touch and attention. This will help calm their fears and know they are a welcomed member of the family.

- *Calming environment.* Dogs, especially puppies, become overwhelmed when there is a lot of chaos. They don't know what to do or how to handle it. This can make them act out, causing other problems.

- *Their space.* Just like people, dogs need their space. They need an area they can call their own. This is an area where they should feel safe and can have some dog time, just like humans need "me time."

- *They need supervision.* If you have a child and get a puppy, you will find a lot of common characteristics between the two, especially if you have a toddler and a puppy. While older dogs don't need as much supervision, a puppy is going to need a lot of attention and supervision. Puppies can become easily wound up and don't understand they can hurt someone if they jump on them. Therefore, watch your pup when they are playing to ensure everyone stays happy and safe.

You Need to Exercise Your Dog

If you are not one for walking, jogging or running, you will need to think about a dog walker or start exercising. Dogs need a lot of exercise, including walking every day. Dogs will need room so they can run, play, and jump. Therefore, you should always think twice about having a large dog in a small apartment where they rarely get to go outside.

Fortunately, if you are not one for exercise but still want a dog, there are breeds of dogs that require little exercise. For example, senior dogs will still need to go outside for a walk, but they are tamer and have lost a lot of energy. Smaller dogs are often okay to have if you are not huge on outdoor exercise because your home will give them room to play around and exercise.

Most Dogs Live for 10 Years or More

When you choose a dog, you want to keep in mind that you will most likely have this dog for over a decade. While this is usually a plus when it comes to picking a dog, some people are not interested in having a dog for years for various reasons. If this is the case, one of the best steps to take is to adopt an older dog. While you will need to factor in health problems, they might be the best choice if you only want a dog for a few years.

At the same time, you might want a dog who is known for a long lifespan. For example, you are getting a dog for your 10-year-old child to teach them responsibility. It takes years for most children to learn how to be responsible. At the same time, you will want a younger dog because you want your child and the dog to spend years together.

Most Dogs Require Grooming

The amount of grooming your dog needs will vary depending on the breed. Some dogs tend to need their fur trimmed often, while the fur on other breeds is fine without trimming. If you have a short-haired dog, you won't need to send them to the groomers as often. However, long-haired dogs require regular grooming and everyday brushing.
All dogs will need to get a bath from time to time. You need to wash their coat with special soap that is not only safe for the dogs, but also valuable for their fur. Along with fur comes shedding. Most dog breeds shed, but short-haired dogs are going to shed more than long-haired dogs.

A Puppy Doesn't Stay Small Forever

Puppies are adorable. Most people seem to want a puppy for several reasons. They are small, will lay in your lap, playful, and silly. Unfortunately, puppies do not stay small forever. Before you decide on a puppy because of its size, do a little research on the breed to see how big they can grow. Even puppies who seem on the smaller side for their breed can grow into large dogs. Don't let the adorable puppy size fool you!

Can You Meet the Parents?

Some people, especially people who want a show dog, will only take home a puppy if they can meet the puppy's parents. While this might not be important to you, it is something to consider if you have children, want to train your dog to become a show dog, or simply want to meet the parents. Parents can tell you a lot about how your puppy could grow up. But you always need to remember, a lot of your dog's temperament is going to deal with how you treat them.

Choosing the Best Breed for Training

It's true, some dogs are easily trainable. If you know that you will train your dog and don't want too many struggles with it, you will want to look at breeds that are easy to train.

What Makes a Dog Easily Trainable?

There are many factors that you need to think of when looking for an easily trainable dog.

- *Are they easily distracted?* Some dogs are more distractible than other dogs. For example, if you want a dog for hunting, you will not want to get a dog that is going to get distracted by leaves rustling in the trees or blowing in the wind. This can cause you to lose your target. You want a dog that is going to be aware of their surroundings yet stays focused on its target. Strong concentration also helps when you are training. Your dog will stay focused on what you are telling them and your hand signals.
- *What is the dog's personality?* Each breed has a distinct personality. Of course, each dog is a bit different than the others, but each breed has certain personality characteristics.

For example, some breeds are going to cooperate better than other breeds.

- *What is the dog's instinct drives?* Each breed has certain instincts that drive them. This means these drives take over the dog's other instincts. For example, bloodhounds are ruled by their nose. Therefore, what they hear and see at the same time they are smelling something is not going to matter as much.

Best Breeds for Training

Miniature Schnauzer

As members of the Terrier group, Miniature Schnauzer's are not considered easily trainable dogs. This is because most Terrier dogs are harder to train than other breeds. However, Miniature Schnauzer's enjoy pleasing their owners and will work hard to accomplish a task. They are fearless, playful, and have a better trainability rate than any other dog in the Terrier family.

These small dogs can go anywhere you are. They can roam around on a farm in the country or remain content in an apartment. They have a spunky personality and make people laugh with their human-like expressions. Miniature Schnauzer gets along well with other dogs and children. They tend to make great watchdogs.

Doberman Pinscher

The Doberman Pinscher is a loyal and fearless companion. They are one of the breeds that are used for police and military training. They listen well, have great attention to detail, and the ability to concentrate on a task. Doberman Pinschers understand their commands, are quick to learn, and retain a lot of information.

Doberman Pinschers are not commonly chosen to be companions because they have a stereotype of being ruthless and known to attack. In reality, these dogs are cuddly, love to play, and friendly. They will only attack when they are threatened, like most dogs, or are trained and told to attack.

Doberman owners are honest about the stereotype their companions deal with on a daily basis. Walking your Doberman down the street, you start to notice people crossing the street ahead of you. They are watching how close you get as they cross. A few minutes later, you sit on a park bench to get a frisbee out of your bag. The guy next to you says, "I heard those dogs would attack their owner after their brain stops growing. Aren't you afraid of that dog attacking your neck?" You look at the person, get down on your knees, and say, "Come here, come give me a hug." You Doberman companion gently places both of their front paws on your shoulder, and you embrace them in a hug. Looking back at the person you say, "Not at all. They are big teddy bears."

Andrew Wildesen wrote an article dedicated to the stereotype Doberman Pinschers and their owners face. Wildesen stated that Dobermans are similar to every other dog–they can be trained to attack. However, they won't innately attack. Instead, they will bring more love and happiness into your life. Wildesen states, "The true Doberman is a lover with loads of enthusiasm… They are goofy and are guaranteed to make you laugh… they are tremendously loyal and love to cuddle… yes, Dobermans… are serious CUDDLE BUGS!" (Wildesen, n.d.).

One of the factors to be aware of with a Doberman is you need to put a lot of effort into their training. If you are looking for a dog that is easily trainable but doesn't require a lot of time, you will want to look at a different breed. You need to provide constant leadership and training for the Doberman breed to thrive.

Poodle

Poodles are common dogs chosen for many reasons. First, they are smaller in size, allowing them to adapt to various types of living situations. Poodles come in three different sizes: toy, miniature, and standard. Second, they are typically energetic and great with kids. Third, they are on every list that describes easily trainable dogs.

People love to train Poodles because they are extremely smart. However, some owners say they are too smart for their own good as they are known to outwit their trainers! They learn their tricks quickly and are eager to please their owner. It doesn't matter what size of Poodle you choose, they will all do their best to surprise you with the tricks you teach them.

Rottweiler

The Rottweiler breed is similar to Doberman Pinschers. They are known for their aggressive nature, but it is all in their training. On top of this, Rottweilers are easily trainable dogs because it is in their nature. In fact, they crave training and it is essential for their happiness.

Rottweilers are great to use as service and police dogs. However, they not only need basic training, they also need social training. This type of training goes beyond sitting and shaking hands as they like to be challenged.

German Shepherd

The German Shepherd is the Jack-of-all-trades dog. They are easy to train because they understand commands. They remember the tricks they are taught and need jobs to keep themselves happy. Furthermore, they are willing to learn and want to please you. They will go above and beyond the call of duty. German Shepherds tend to work tirelessly and are great for military and police work.

Like most dogs, German Shepherds need a lot of exercises. You will need to keep their mind going as well as their body. You don't need to wait too long to start training these dogs. They can understand the basic commands as young as eight weeks old.

Havanese

Another dog that does great with apartment living is the Havanese. They are highly intelligent, making them easily trainable. Furthermore, these dogs are full of energy and love the outdoors. This means that you will need to make sure your Havanese can get outside to let run off some of their energy. At the same time, because of their smaller size, they will get a lot of running done indoors.

Like most other dogs, the Havanese's coat needs to be brushed a couple of times a week. They don't tend to shed, so are great hypoallergenic dogs. When training a Havanese, positive reinforcement is your best procedure. They are sensitive dogs and quickly understand your tone of voice. Once they realize the tones, they will judge how you feel about them and their actions by your tone.

Shetland Sheepdog

The Shetland Sheepdog is a competitive dog. They enjoy dog sports, are playful, and affectionate. They love learning new behaviors as it keeps their mind and body active. If you have a Shetland Sheepdog, you should enroll them in obedience or agility classes because they will thrive with this additional training. Like the German Shepherds, Shetland Sheepdogs want to please people. This causes them to work hard to learn new tasks. Because of their high intelligence, they learn and retain new information easily.

Shetland Sheepdogs are great to have in the country but can adapt to apartment living. However, they are extremely active and can grow about 13 to 16 inches at the shoulder when standing. They are sensitive dogs and don't tend to bark unless they feel danger or a stranger is approaching. Therefore, they make great watchdogs.

The Papillon Club

The Papillon is an active little dog who needs to be kept busy. They don't get much taller than 11 inches at the shoulder. If you choose this breed, you will want to think about an active training schedule. The training you give the Papillon should mentally motivate them as well as physically. They are curious dogs and quick to learn.
Unlike some breeds, the Papillon learns from each experience, and they remember everything. Therefore, you need to maintain consistency as a trainer. If you are not consistent, your Papillon is not going to thrive. They will become confused and seem like they lack skills, including potty training.

Border Terrier

Border Terriers are a smaller dog that can easily adapt to any living situation. While they are not the most popular dogs, they are great dogs for families. They love children, love to learn, and great dogs for training. Because border terriers enjoy agility classes, they are perfect dogs for easy training.

Australian Shepherd

The Australian Shepherd is a medium-sized dog, which makes apartment living a bit of a challenge for them. They don't like to spend a lot of time indoors. Australian Shepherds thrive best when they have a large area to run around, play, and learn.
Australian Shepherds are known for their herding instincts. For example, many people will train them for herding sheep or cows from one pasture to the other. However, some owners have also found their dogs trying to herd a group of children. The dogs will not hurt the children, but younger children can become confused and frightened when an Australian Shepherd is trying to herd them into a designated area.
The best home for an Australian shepherd is with someone who can devote a lot of time in training them. They are dogs that need a lot of love and a firm voice to keep them in line. They can lose sight of what they are supposed to do because of their boundless energy.

While some breeds are fine with training starting later in life, Australian Shepherds need to start as puppies. They are happy when their owners take time to train them and can work off much of their energy.

Golden Retriever

The Golden Retriever is one of the most popular breeds. They are known for their beauty and hunting skills. They are also used as seeing-eye dogs and for search and rescue missions. They are willing to learn and enjoy competitive events. A Golden Retriever is a dog that you would enroll in an obedience class because they enjoy this type of setting.

Golden Retrievers are family dogs that are eager to please. They are highly intelligent, making them easily trainable. They have a happy and playful approach to life, making them energetic and powerful dogs for outdoor activities. Because they are a medium-sized dog, they don't enjoy apartment life well. However, if you make sure they exercise daily and take them outside, they will do fine in an apartment.

Where to Go?

Now that you are briefed on some of the most trainable dog breeds, you might be asking yourself where to go. Thanks to the internet and social media, the places you can find a dog of your choosing is right at your fingertips.

Adoption

One of the first places to go is a local animal shelter or rescue group. There are a variety of dogs you can find in a shelter. Some places are mainly for purebreds, but most take in any dogs that need a place to stay until they are adopted.

One of the biggest challenges for people when adopting a dog is the unknown history and how to make the dog comfortable in their new home. To help your dog adjust to their new life, here are a few tips to follow.

- *Don't expect too much right away.* The new member of your family needs time to adjust. You shouldn't start to train them right away. Your main focus for the first few days to a couple of weeks is making them comfortable.

- *Understand they have emotional trauma.* Most dogs that come from a shelter have some type of emotional trauma, and you need to help them heal. This is going to take time. The dog was abandoned or got lost. They don't understand what happened to their companion, who they still love and miss. Plus, their time in the shelter can cause emotional damage, even if they were treated well. Be patient as you work through this trauma with them; it will take years to repair. Unfortunately, some trauma will remain with the dog.

- *The dog might act differently in the shelter.* If you come across a dog you fall in love with, but they act scared and bark a lot doesn't mean they will act this way in your home. The shelter makes them anxious, causing them to react in this way. Don't believe they will always act in that way. Once you bring them home and they become comfortable, the dog will relax and act typical for their breed.

- *Start a routine right away.* One way to help the dog feel comfortable in their new environment is to establish a routine immediately. This doesn't mean you start training them right away. Instead, you will feed them at a regular time, show them where their water is, place their bed in a certain area, go to bed at a specific time, get up at a regular time, and play with them. If you struggle with routines yourself, get a planner and what down what to do when with your new dog. Be as consistent as possible because they will start to trust what is happening next. If their routine changes, it can make them anxious.

Pet Store

I won't deny this—there is a lot of debate about pet stores. Some pet stores do receive dogs from puppy mills, but not all. Do thorough research on your pet store before you decide to get a dog there. Go to visit the possible animal a couple of times and get to know the employees. While they can't hold the dog you are interested in for you, knowing the background of the store will help you understand the dog better.

Some pet store will advertise that they are "puppy friendly," meaning they don't use puppy mills as a resource. While this can be true, remember anything can be said through advertising. Through research, you should find out where the puppies come from as some stores do take homeless dogs.

Responsible Breeders

Some people breed dogs. These dogs are usually purebred and well taken care of. Of course, you will still want to get to know the breeders. If you can, talk to other people who have gotten puppies from them. Interview the breeders and get to know the breeders. Ask them why they decided to breed and how long they've had the parents.

Social Media

There are a lot of social media sites that will sell puppies. Usually, the people have a dog that became pregnant and they can't care for all the puppies. Sometimes they are giving away the dogs and sometimes asking for money. Typically, they don't ask for a lot of money, but it depends on the breed. If you feel that they are asking too much for the dog, do a little research. They might be part of a puppy mill.

You always want to be cautious of online social media sales. While most occur locally, there are people willing to ship the dog if you send the money to them. This can easily be a scam, just like any smaller business stating the same thing. Always do your research if you don't know the people.

Tips to Keep in Mind Before Bringing Your Dog Home

It is always a bit challenging for some of us to say we are searching for our "best" dog. If you love dogs and want to take one home, you are going to be fine with getting a free puppy out of a cardboard box from your neighbor's home. Of course, there is nothing wrong with this. But, for many people, finding the best dog is necessary for several reasons. Whether you are looking at your neighbor's new litter of puppies or thinking of heading to the animal shelter, here are a few tips to help you along the way.

Be Cautious of Internet Sites

You are searching online for your Australian Shepherd. You know there isn't an Australian Shepherd available locally. However, you notice this small business called "Worldwide Love For Dogs Rescue." As you read about the newly established company, you come to learn that they will talk to you through video chat where you can see your potential dog. You can also receive email information about your dog's personality before making the final purchase. Then, once you send them the money, they will transport your dog to you. Sounds like a pretty good deal if you find the perfect Australian Shepherd for your home, right? This can be a good deal, but it can also be a scam.

One factor to consider is what do you really know about the company? You should always read up on any reviews, whether they are positive or negative. Do a little research on the company. Are they establish as an LLC or another type of organization? You can often find this information online. Do they keep their business clean? Another factor to consider is how well they treat their dogs. People can easily tell you how they treat animals in a way that makes you believe they take care of their dogs. But you never truly know until you see the dog or do a little research on the company.

It is always a good idea to do a background check on the person you are thinking of doing business with. While you might have to pay for a background check, there is information you can find for free through research. Remember, people can say anything in advertising. No one is going to tell you that they have 125 dogs caged in unsanitary conditions because they are running a puppy mill or into dog fighting.

Visit the Dog on Site

Another reason many people will caution anyone against getting a dog through an online store where they are shipped is because visiting the dog on site is 100% helpful. There are hardly any downsides to visiting the dog before you decide to take them home. The only real downside is you are going to fall in love with the dog and have to wait until any paperwork and your background check clears or you will fall in love with all the dogs and can't bring them all home!

Seeing where the dog sleeps and temporarily lives will allow you to understand the dog. You will see firsthand how well they eat and interact with other people and animals. You will also make the dog more comfortable when you bring them home. Dogs can be nervous when they are chosen as they don't understand what is happening. While they might seem excited, like any animal, they will be cautious of their new surroundings and home. Meeting the dog in their home can help them feel more comfortable during transportation and their new living situation.

Poor Breeding Practices and Living Conditions

Visiting the site will help you see how well the dog's temporary residence is taken care of. If you walk into a building and see dozens or hundreds of dogs, some that are kept in the same cage, the building smells bad, and the dogs seems scared, ungroomed, thin, and not cared for (i.e., water might be dirty or water bowl empty) you might be in the middle of a puppy mill situation. It's important to note that animal shelters have standards they need to ensure they follow. Puppy mills are typically illegal and aren't kept up to standards.

If you ever find yourself in this situation, the best step to take is to try to get some background information. Are they running an animal shelter that is registered as a business? Closely check the conditions of the dogs. If you notice they don't give you a lot of information or don't answer your questions, contact the police department or a local animal welfare agency. It's always better to ensure that the dogs are well taken care of than to allow a puppy mill to continue.

While you might want to get one of the puppies to bring home for a better life, you need to be aware that dogs from puppy mills are often sick. They can carry diseases from the unsanitary conditions and need to be taken to a veterinarian immediately.

Chapter 2

E-Collar Basics

When you look at the instructions for an e-collar, you may feel confident you have all the information you need. Unfortunately, you are wrong. While companies give you detailed instructions when you purchase their e-collar, it can still be confusing for many reasons. First, each breed is going to react differently to the e-collar. This will happen because of their personality and how trainable they are. For example, some dogs will struggle with the e-collar because they are more independent and don't care to please their owners like other breeds. Second, each button is going to make the dog feel a different way, making your dog react in different ways to the e-collar. This can throw you off as you fear you might be doing something wrong.

Don't allow the way your dog reacts to the buttons throw you off. This is going to throw your dog off as well. Dogs can sense how you feel. For example, if you push a button on the e-collar and you notice them take a step back, you start to feel worried you hurt them. Your dog will sense this, causing them more uneasiness with the e-collar and training in general.

What Is the E-Collar?

A little over 30 years ago, the first electric dog collar made an appearance. Initially used to train hunting dogs, people became excited and worried about how the collar affected their dog. Some people felt they are harmful while other people believed they are a great training tool. The first e-collar only delivered one stimulation level. Today, there are three stimulation levels–high, medium, and low–and various levels of intensity within these stimulation levels for many e-collars. It is safe to say that over the last three decades, e-collars are safer, made for all types of dogs, and a perfect training tool.

The e-collar is a collar that has a radio receiver attached to it. The radio will receive a signal from the transmitter. This signal will give your dog a small electrical shock, similar to how you feel static electricity. This startles your dog enough to know that what they are doing is not appropriate. Over time, you will train your dog through the e-collar to know what behavior is right and wrong.

Most people choose e-collars because they don't want to train their dog with a leash. Another reason people choose e-collars is that they can train their dog from a small distance. For example, you are at the park with your dog when they start running off. Instead of yelling at your dog, you press a button. This alerts your dog to stop running and come back to you. Of course, at this point you have trained your dog to respond to the shock by looking at you to see what you want. For instance, you will motion them to come back. If you want them to sit, you will motion them to sit.

You can purchase a e-collar in most stores or online. If you've never worked with an e-collar, you might want to go to your local pet store. The employees there will help you understand how the e-collar works and answer any questions you have.

Types of E-Collars

When searching for the best e-collar for your dog, you need to think of why you're training. E-collar aren't always used for basic training, but some are focused for yard use. There are also e-collars for hunting, no barking, and working dogs.

Yard Training

Yard training e-collars is mainly for your pets, but some can be used for other training purposes. They are some of the most common e-collars and give you a lot of options.

- *EZ 900 Easy Educator* is an e-collar that focuses on safety for your dog. Its boosting level reaches to 60 and stimulation level to 100. It's considered the most humane e-collar on the market. This e-collar is a smaller size, making it great for any size dog. Many people who purchased this product say you won't see the typical head jerking coming from your dog. You can use the EZ 900 up to ½ a mile and can be used for hunting and working training as well. Another benefit of this collar is it's one of the cheaper ones on the market.
- *ET-302 Zen Educator* is another humane collar that can reach about a ½ mile. The stimulation level reaches to 100 and holds boosting levels from 1 to 60. It includes a collar to help you find your dog in the dark and is waterproof. This collar is sized for any dog and has two receivers, but is specifically for yard use.
- *ET-402 Educator* has stimulation levels from 1 to 100 and boosting levels from 1 to 60. This e-collar can reach up to ¾ of a mile and is great for emergency situations. It's

waterproof and includes a light. Any size dog can wear this collar, but it's specific to yard training.
- The *FT-330 Finger Trainer Educator* is one of the newer models that can reach up to ½ a mile. It's a smaller collar, but holds enough stimulation for any sized dog. This collar holds most of the same specifics of the other collars, but includes a remote finger button.
- *ME-300 Micro Educator* works best for smaller dogs. It's a smaller version of the RX-090 Mini Educator Receiver but holds the same features. Its range is a ⅓ mile and charges quicker than other e-collars.

Hunting Training

While a few yard training e-collars are used for hunting as well, many professionals feel it's better to get a specific hunting collar.
- *UL-1200 Upland Dog Trainer* is one of the cheaper hunting e-collars, but it's also older than some models. Its stimulation and boosting levels are the same as other e-collars. You won't want to use this e-collar on smaller dogs because of its size. One benefit of this e-collar is it can be used for yard and working training as well.
- *WF-1202 Waterfowler* is a perfect hunting training e-collar. It's the best on the market and can reach up to one mile. While this e-collar is useful for any type of training, it's only for medium and large dogs.

Work Training

Work training e-collars are perfect for dogs with certain jobs and performances. They are sometimes used in seeing-eye dog training or dogs preparing for dog shows.

- *ET-802 Dog Remote Trainer* is a newer version of the ET-800 Dog Remote Trainer. It holds the same type of stimulation and boosting levels as other e-collars. This e-collar is usable for any type of training, but only used on medium or large dogs. It's weight and size is too much for a smaller dog to handle. It can reach up to one mile.
- The *K9-402 K9 Handler* can reach up to ¾ of a mile. It's one of the smallest working dog training e-collars, making it perfect for any sized dog. You can also use this e-collar for yard or hunting training.
- *Pro Educator 900* is an older e-collar built with safety in mind. It's smaller in size, so perfect for any type of dog. It reaches up to ½ a mile and is also great to use as a no-bark collar.

No-Bark E-Collar

There aren't a lot of e-collars specific for no barking as you can typically use any type of e-collar for this training. However, the main no bark e-collar is the *BP-504 Anti Bark Collar*. It's newer on the market, has nine stimulation levels and three sensitivity levels. This e-collar is great for no barking because it comes with a warning sound your dog will quickly understand. This e-collar should not be used for any dog under five pounds.

E-Collar Accessories

Each e-collar will come with a manual and it's necessary pieces, such as the transmitter, battery charger, lanyard, contact point tool, e-collar, strap, and extra contact points. You can also purchase various accessories to go with your e-collar. For instance, many people like to purchase another contact point tool as it allows for more than one person to control the dog. As long as you are both on the same page, this won't confuse your dog. You just want to ensure that you are both aware of what type of training you're focusing on. Other accessories include:

- A carrying case for all your dog training tools. Some people don't keep the e-collar on their dog as it's only for training purposes. For example, if you are training your dog to hunt, you don't need to have the e-collar on your dog when you're at home.

- A dummy e-collar. Some people purchase this accessory because it makes your dog believe the collar is still on when it's charging. If you are not constantly training your dog, this isn't necessary unless you want to test your dog on their training.

- The Educator Gear Keeper is great for anyone who is training their dog on the go. You can attach this device to your belt loop or purse to give you quick access. It allows you to put away the transmitter instead of keeping it in your hand constantly.

- Educator bungee straps are popular because they come in a variety of colors. They come in 33-inch and 37-inch lengths but can be cut down to size. They are also extremely comfortable for your dog and easy to clean. Unfortunately, they are not the best for smaller dogs.

How to Use an E-Collar

E-collars are not meant to be used as a source of punishment. They are meant to deter the dog from unsafe and negative behavior. The purpose is an e-collar will train the dog that their negative behavior gives them an uncomfortable shock. The dog will remember this sock and stop the behavior. This theory will only work if you don't allow your dog to know you control the collar and you allow them to become comfortable with the collar.

Parts and Terminology

- Stimulation level. The best e-collars to get are the ones that have at least 100 levels of stimulation. The more levels you have, the easier it is to train and select the best shock for your dog.
- Power Output. Do not assume that larger dogs need a higher stimulation level. Dog trainers often find lower stimulation levels are great for dogs over 100 pounds. At the same time, your smaller dog might need a higher level. It's difficult to find the "sweet spot" for stimulation, but by paying attention to your dog's reaction and talking to a professional trainer, if necessary, it's 100% possible.
- Vibrate or tone. Find an e-collar that allows you to emit a collar vibration or audible tone. These are used as warning signs that the shock is going to happen. What typically happens is that your dog will start to notice the tone or vibration and stop the behavior immediately, so a shock isn't needed.
- Distance. It is helpful to get an e-collar with considerable distance. A ¼ of a mile is minimum and a mile is usually

maximum. The average length is ½ mile and perfect for house training. If you are more interested in hunting, you will find e-collars with one-mile distance.

Step One: Read the Instructions

Every e-collar should come with instructions. If you purchase a e-collar from a thrift store, garage sale, or a third party you can easily find instructions online. It is essential that you follow the instructions given to you. You always want to read the instructions before you put the e-collar together and attach it to your dog.

Step Two: Place the Batteries Into the Transmitter

Your transmitter is your remote. You will use this to control the e-collar, telling it when to give your dog a little shock. You want to ensure that the e-collar works with the transmitter and the levels aren't too high for your dog. You can do this by testing it on yourself first.
It is always best to put the e-collar on its lowest setting to start, even on larger dogs. Many people feel that larger dogs need a higher setting to feel the shock. This isn't necessarily true. Dogs are extremely sensitive to the shock they are given, no matter what their size. While a small dog will feel a stronger shock from a larger e-collar, bigger dogs can feel the same type of shock as a small dog from a smaller e-collar. Another reason to place the e-collar on the lowest setting is so you don't accidentally shock your dog when fitting the collar.

Step Three: Fit the E-Collar on Your Dog's Neck

With the e-collar turned off or on the lowest setting, fit the collar on your dog. Make sure that you can place your pointer and middle finger between the collar and your dog's neck. This is the general rule of thumb for any collar to ensure that it's not on too tight.

Be aware of e-collars that have small prongs. These have to touch the dog's neck, but you don't want to make it uncomfortable. You might need to adjust the e-collar a couple of times once you use it before you find the best fit.

One of the biggest mistakes is putting the e-collar too low. A dog's neck is shaped bigger at the base of their neck, causing the e-collar to move up the neck when they start playing. Here are some tips for fitting the e-collar:

- If your dog has thick fur, de-shed their neck first.
- Place the e-collar high on your dog's neck, but not at the top.
- Use two fingers to ensure it is a snug fit, but not too tight.
- Rotate the e-collar every couple of hours so your dog's neck doesn't get irritated by the collar.

Step Four: Let Your Dog Adjust to the E-Collar for a Week

While this step is optional, many professionals say it's best to not use the e-collar for a week. This will let your dog get used to the collar before it feels the first shock and not associate it with punishment. The point of the e-collar is to make the dog believe the negative behavior is causing the shock. If the dog knows it's the e-collar, the training can become difficult and they can try to escape from the collar.

Step Five: Start Using the E-Collar

Start with the lowest stimulation level and observe your dog's actions. If they react, such as moving their head or twitching their ears, keep the level low. If they don't react, upgrade the level. The dog should never whimper or try to run away because of a shock. If your dog makes noise like they are hurt, the shock is too strong and you need to lower the levels. If they're at the lowest level, you need to find a smaller e-collar for your dog.

Always be consistent when using the e-collar for training. For example, you don't want your dog jumping on the furniture, use the e-collar every time you see them do this. They might still do it when you aren't looking, but if you are consistent they will learn not to jump.

Step Six: Start with Commands Your Dog Understands

Your dog should already know basic training tricks, such as sitting. When first using the e-collar, start by saying commands they understand. If they don't respond, use the e-collar to get their attention. When the shock is received, repeat the command. Don't do this repeatedly over a few minutes as this can stress out your dog. Follow this step whenever you want your dog to sit, stay, or lay down. Every time your dog responds remember to praise them.

Step Seven: Control Your Dog's Negative Behavior

After your dog responds to basic commands, use the e-collar to control their negative behavior. For instance, if your dog jumps on company, use the e-collar every time you see them jump. While many people find their dog's growling or barking annoying, don't shock them immediately. Remember, this is how dogs communicate when something seems wrong to them. If they are barking because a stranger is coming toward your home, think about if shocking them is the best choice. Dogs are territorial and have natural protective instincts. You don't want to silence these instincts.

Do your best to ensure your dog doesn't see you using the transmitter. They are smart animals and will connect the shock to your transmitter. If they see you shocking them for their behavior, they will start distrusting you. You want your dog to believe the shock happens because of the negative behavior and not you.

E-Collar Safety

Don't Leave Your Dog Unattended with an E-Collar

Most people believe that you should have the e-collar on your dog, but this isn't necessarily safe. Your best step is to purchase the dummy e-collar and place this on your dog when you aren't training them, during the night, or when they are home alone. There is always a possibility that the e-collar will overcorrect or malfunction. While this is rare, it can harm your dog if it happens. Of course, because this is a rare occurrence, it is up to you.

Understand Your E-Collar

One of the best ways to practice safety with the e-collar is to ensure you understand everything about the e-collar. You have a vast amount of knowledge and know how to use your transmitter before you begin training. For example, you understand what all the buttons do and are prepared to follow your dog's reaction to know when the e-collar is at the right stimulation level.

Don't Use a Leash with the E-Collar

Using a leash with the e-collar can cause the front of the collar to push up against the dog's neck if the leash is pulled one way or another. If you shock them at the same time, this can harm them. You can use a harness that is attached to the leash, but don't attach any part of the leash or harness to the e-collar.

Don't Use the E-Collar When Your Dog is Swimming

While e-collars are waterproof, it's safer to keep them out of the water. If your dog is going to swim, remove the e-collar and don't replace it until their neck is dry. Following this rule not only secures your dog's safety but can make you e-collar last longer. When you need to wash the e-collar, always use warm and soapy water.

Benefits of an E-Collar

Fast Results

One of the challenges of training is that people don't have the time or patience to effectively train their dog. However, people who use the e-collar state it provides fast results and only takes a few shocks for the dog to stop the negative behavior. This works because before the dog feels the jolt, they will feel the warning vibration, associating this warning to the shock. Therefore, feeling the vibration makes them stop the behavior so you don't have to give them a shock.

Unfortunately, not everyone has had the quick success rates. Dogs that are stubborn tend to be harder to train. If you don't have an easily trainable canine, you shouldn't expect quick results.

Long Lasting Behavioral Changes

Professional trainers say e-collar training is the best way to change your dog's behavior, as long as it's used correctly. Studies have proved that dogs remember the behavior that brought on the shock better than a tone of voice or any other type of training technique. Hunting dogs trained not to go too close to the sheep received a shock. A year later, the dogs returned for another test and demonstrated hesitation when they started wandering too close to the sheep, proving they remember the shock when they got too close to the sheep. In fact, only one out of 114 dogs required a shock during the return test (Evans, 2018).

E-Collars Don't Take a Lot of Strength

When you use a leash for training, you need to have a tight grip and remain strong, especially with bigger dogs. They can easily pull a person around if you aren't strong enough to handle your dog. Strength isn't a concern with the e-collar because you use the transmitter to give the dog a warning noise or vibration and then a shock if their behavior doesn't change. Your dog can even be a ¼ of a mile away from you and still feel the warning and shock.

You Don't Stress Your Voice

Most dog owners know the stress your voice can feel when your dog doesn't listen to you, especially when their safety is concerned. For example, your dog escapes from their leash and runs into the street. Your automatic reaction is to yell at the top of your lungs for your dog to come back so they aren't hit by a driver. This can damage your vocal cords if you aren't careful or find yourself yelling often. With the e-collar, you don't need to say a word. You simply press the button and the e-collar does the rest.

Yelling or speaking to your dog angrily can cause them to become stressed, affecting them emotionally. They will become confused about what exactly they did wrong and worry about what will happen next. This poor communication between you and your dog can change with the e-collar. First, if you properly train them, they won't associate you to the e-collar. This will make them more comfortable with you. Second, your dog will receive clear communication in their current behavior by giving them a shock. They will come to understand that this behavior is unpleasant, making them stop.

E-Collars Allow for Easier Consistency

Training your dog with a leash or voice is difficult. Some people are afraid to train their dog in public using their voice for fear of causing a scene or judgment. The e-collar allows you to train your dog wherever you are without people realizing you are shocking your dog unless they see you push the button. If you do struggle with social anxiety and still worry what people will say or do when they learn you use an e-collar, you can purchase small transmitter to fit onto your belt or in your purse and push the button more discreetly. However, this should not become an issue because most people understand e-collars do not harm dogs.

Your Dog Receives Off-Leash Freedom

Leashes keep dogs in a certain area. While you can get a long leash, this can cause problems with your dog wrapping themselves around a tree or another object. Furthermore, if people aren't fully paying attention they can trip over the leash. E-collars will give your dog the freedom of running and playing without the tug of the leash. It is also safer as your dog can't tangle themselves up or trip anyone.

Common Myths About the E-Collar

The e-collar received a lot of criticism when it first became public. People automatically saw the e-collar as a harmful device for their companion. After all, who would want to shock their dog in order to teach them right from wrong? People who used e-collars were asked, "How would you feel if I shocked you when you did something wrong?" The harm an e-collar can cause a dog soon became a myth that still exists today.

The Shocks Harm Your Dog

Before I go too far into the world of e-collars, I want to tell you that the shocks your dog receives will not harm them. I love my dogs and have used e-collars for years. My dogs have never shown any signs of harm from the e-collars. Like you, I did a lot of research before I finally found the e-collar for my dogs. Since I purchased the e-collar, I will not go back to any other training technique. If my dogs ever showed signs of the collar hurting them, I would have stopped using it in a heartbeat. The shocks the dogs receive are similar to a static shock. While they are not fun to receive, they don't harm you.

If you take your dog to a training class that uses e-collars, they might have you try the e-collar yourself. I did this when I received the e-collar. I became surprised by the shock and felt more comfortable using it because it did not hurt me in any way. Therefore, I knew it wouldn't hurt my dogs.

Only Professional Trainers Can Use E-collars

Some people believe e-collars are difficult to use. While e-collars were difficult to use when they first came out, technology has changed. Today, they are easy to use. You don't need to be a professional trainer or talk to a professional to use e-collars.

The E-Collar Burns Your Dog

The e-collar does not burn the dog. There is no way that the e-collar can burn any dog because it does not get hot. The e-collar does not give off any type of heat when it gently shocks your dog.

The E-Collar Leaves Marks On the Dog's Neck

If you do see any marks from the e-collar, they are pressure marks. You have to rotate the e-collar on your dog at least every four hours. Furthermore, you should ensure you can place two fingers between your dog's collar and their neck. If you can't fit two fingers, the collar is too tight, making the e-collar uncomfortable for your companion.

Chapter 3

Your Dog and Their E-Collar

Before you choose an e-collar, you need to know why you want the training tool. For example, are you going to train your dog at home, for hunting, or to stop them from barking. The type of training goals you have depend on what e-collar you will get. At the same time, you need to remember your dog's size as not all e-collars fit well for smaller dogs.

Choosing the Best E-Collar

One of the toughest decisions you will make when e-collar training is what e-collar to buy for your dog. The list of e-collars in Chapter 2 should give you an idea of what to look for, depending on your training goals. For example, if you are going to house train, you want to focus on yard training e-collars.

The Fundamental Five

One way to help you choose the best e-collar is to follow these five tips.
1. *Choose an e-collar you can count on*

    Don't buy the cheapest e-collar for your training that you can find. You want to find an e-collar that is waterproof and has great reviews. Take time in looking for the best e-collar and check out online reviews on the product. Compare and contrast the reviews with different type of e-collars. This will help you narrow your decision a little more.
2. *Education is always number one*

Some of the best e-collars on the market will not only come with instructions but also training videos. You always want to focus on e-collars that show they are meant to train your dog and not punish your dog. Always remember, the e-collar is not a shortcut for training. It is a technique to help your dog understand that certain behavior is unwanted effectively and efficiently.

3. *Know your options when it comes to e-collars*

Do as much research as you feel necessary to reach a complete understanding of e-collars. This means you want to research your dog's breed and how they handle training, know that your dog's age is going to affect training, and understand that some dogs are stubborn and will require longer training. This doesn't mean you aren't doing your job as their trainer, it's part of their personality. Look for an e-collar that holds constant and nick options and allows you to switch between the two easily.

4. *Choose an e-collar you understand*

Some e-collars are more complicated to use than others. You don't want to pick an e-collar that will frustrate you. Pick an e-collar that doesn't have a lot of buttons as this means you need to look for the right button to press. By the time you find the button, the teaching moment is gone and your dog won't understand their previous action warranted the shock. They will relate the shock to their current action. Another method is to choose a small transmitter that you can fit in your pocket or clip to your belt for easy and quick access.

5. *Pick a collar only your dog can activate*

There are e-collars that other dogs can activate, especially if you are using a no bark collar. When your dog receives a shock that wasn't meant for them at the time, they will become confused and unsure of why that happened, especially if they were listening, laying down, or sleeping. The best e-collars to purchase are the ones that will only set off a shock if it comes from the dog wearing the collar.

Your Dog's Reaction to the E-Collar

I have mentioned a bit about what to watch out for before, but I want to take this time to thoroughly explain your dog's reaction to the e-collar.

First, the e-collar can distress your dog. This is always a possibility and one that can happen even before you shock your dog for the first time. One of the best tips when it comes to knowing how your dog is going to react to the e-collar is to understand your dog before you even buy an e-collar. For example, if your dog came from a rescue shelter and is easily frightened, the possibility of your dog becoming scared by the e-collar is high. This isn't going to help the training situation, especially when they receive a shock.

Another way to know how your dog might react to the e-collar is to place a different collar on your dog. This is a good idea for dogs that don't have a collar. You will understand how they react to a regular collar and if you will need to speak to a trainer for the best advice on how to introduce your dog to an e-collar.

Unintended Reactions

It is always possible that your dog is going to have reactions you didn't expect to the e-collar. This can happen when they receive their first shock or throughout their training. You might believe you are training them not to leave the yard, when you are really training them to be afraid of someone. Let's look at a couple of case examples so you get a better idea of unintended reactions.

Case Example #1: Tobey and the Neighbor

Tobey is a one-year-old poodle that likes to run over to the neighbor when he sees them outside. While this typically wouldn't be a problem for Tobey's owners, they are concerned for his safety because the neighbor lives across the street. The neighbor is always kind enough to walk Tobey back home, but anything can happen when Tobey sees the neighbor and runs into the street.

Other than the neighbor, Tobey doesn't leave the yard. Therefore, his owners weren't sure that the e-collar would be the best choice to train Tobey not to run out into the street, but they decided it is the best options for Tobey's safety.

Every time they bring Tobey outside, they put the e-collar on him. Every time Tobey ran toward the street because he saw the neighbor, he received a shock. One day, the neighbor came over and as soon as they walked in the door, Tobey bit the neighbor on the leg.

The neighbor and Tobey's owners were shocked by his reaction. They knew he loved to visit the neighbor, so why did he bite them? After speaking to Tobey's trainer, his owners found out that Tobey didn't associate the road to the shock. Instead, he associated the neighbor to the shock. This happened because Tobey's goal was to see the neighbor when he received the shocks. He wasn't thinking about the street or that this was the real cause of the shocks from the collar.

Case Example #2: Donnie and Max

Donnie's parents gave him a seven-month-old puppy named Max for his 10th birthday. The family loved Max, but Donnie's mother worried whenever he took Max for a walk. While she always went with, Donnie held Max's leash. Because Max is an energetic puppy, he often pulled Donnie, especially when he saw another dog.

After talking to her husband, Donnie's parents decided to purchase an e-collar for Max. On their walks, Donnie's mother would shock Max every time he started to pull Donnie. While she felt this worked well at first, she started to notice Max become anxious and aggressive whenever he saw another dog.

One day, Donnie and his mom were walking Max when they met family friends walking their dog. As Donnie and his mom started walking toward their friends, Max stopped and refused to get any closer. Because the family friends felt Max was tired or simply being a puppy, they continued to run up to Donnie and his mother. However, the closer they got, the harder Max tried to go the other way.

"I don't understand why Max started this behavior," Donnie's mother said to Max's trainer. "He always liked meeting dogs before. Now he becomes anxious, growls, and I am afraid he is going to attack another dog one day. What happened?"

"Max didn't associate the shock to pulling Donnie," Max's trainer stated. "He associated another dog with the shock. Therefore, Max believes that if another dog gets too close, he is going to receive a shock."

Dogs are not mind readers. They don't always understand our goals when it comes to their training, such as the case examples show. Both dogs would have received more efficient training without the shock collars. Because Tobey didn't run out into the road unless he saw the neighbor, his owners could have used positive reinforcement to sit on the sidewalk and wait for the neighbor to come over. The same goes for Max, positive reinforcement to not pull Donnie when another dog is spotted would have worked better. You always want to take time to think about what your dog's goals are when they are taking part in unwanted behavior. If they are trying to meet another dog or person, it is best not to shock them because they will associate their mission to the shock.

What If Your Dog Is Scared of the E-Collar

One of the challenges to e-collars you can have is your dog being afraid of the e-collar. This can happen due to two main reasons. First, the dog is frightened of any collar going around his neck. This can happen because of past experiences or because your dog is naturally more fearful than other dogs. Depending on the reason will depend on how you handle the situation. For example, a dog who is naturally fearful is going to overcome the fear easier than a dog who has a negative past experiences with a collar.

There is a lot of debate when it comes to using an e-collar on a fearful dog. Most people feel you should never use an e-collar on a dog that exhibits a lot of fear because their fear will increase. Other people believe this is one of the many myths about e-collars and if you train the dog correctly, you don't have to worry about their fear.

First, you need to understand where the fear comes from. If they are afraid of collars in general, you want them to get comfortable with a different collar and then work toward the e-collar. Even if you decide to leave the e-collar on for a week or two without delivering any shocks, you should start with a regular collar. Another tip is to introduce the regular collar slowly. For example, let them smell the collar and then sit it aside. Later, bring the collar back to them and set it down next to them. Watch your dog's reaction and if they start to show fear, take the collar away. Go slowly, step by step, until you can place the collar around your dog's neck without them trying to break free from it. Once they wear the collar for a week or two without trying to get rid of the collar, then work them into the e-collar. You might have to go a bit slower with introducing this collar because it is a different collar than the first one, but it will go smoothly after a while.

There is a possibility that your dog will not become comfortable with an e-collar. If your dog is from a shelter, a rescue, or from a pet store they may have terrible memories of collars. This trauma is something that they will never truly get over, just like any trauma a human can face. Always remember, there are other ways to train your dog that don't include the e-collar. Your dog's mental health is more important than any type of training.

Some dogs are fine when you put the e-collar on them and they get used to the collar. However, after you shock them once or twice, they become scared. For example, Robbie is a beagle that is learning how to hunt. His owner put an e-collar on him two weeks ago and has used it twice to get Robbie to come back once he has found the duck. One day, Robbie's owner tones him as a warning the shock is about to occur if he doesn't come back. Instead of heading back, Robbie drops to the ground and doesn't move. Concerned, his owner goes to him and notices he is scared. Robbie looks at his owner and whimpers a little.

A week later, Robbie and his owner are at a training class. His owner explains what happened and asked the trainer what to do. The trainer tell Robbie's owner that he is afraid of the shock. "This happens with some dogs. They understand the tone means a shock can happen and freeze because they don't want the shock and don't know how to protect themselves from it. Beagles aren't the easiest dogs to train with the e-collar for this reason, many tend to become afraid and freeze. Tonight, we can talk about other training methods instead of the e-collar. It's best that you don't use the e-collar unless you absolutely need to."

Your dog can have a lot of reactions to the e-collar. Some dogs are known to become more aggressive when they are shocked. If your dog has a reaction that shows fear or aggression, you should stop using the e-collar immediately. Your dog will respond better to a reward system and leash training. I would start by placing your dog into a training class and discussing any other training techniques with a professional.

The Story of Frankie and her E-Collar

Frankie is a black lab who was taken in by her owners, Amirah and Thomas, because she couldn't become a show dog. She was born without any fur and while her first owners took her to the veterinarian and gave her medicine, fur never grew on the tip of her nose. Thomas, who worked with Frankie's initial owners, learned they were going to send Frankie to the shelter because they only keep show dogs to train and then sell. That's when Thomas said he would buy Frankie for his wife.

When Thomas brought Frankie home, she was seven months old. The couple had read up on how to raise a black lab because they knew she had natural hunting instincts, but they were not hunters.

Amirah and Thomas started the basic training with Frankie, but had a problem with her getting into the garbage. She would get into the garbage on the side of the garage, leaving it all over. Even when the couple caught her, they could barely pull her away from the garbage.

Worried about their dog's health from what she could eat in the garbage and tired of picking up trash all around their yard, they looked into other training methods. After researching the e-collar, they decided to give it a try.

Amirah, who works from home, spent her days training Frankie and followed the e-collar instructions. She let Frankie wear the collar for a week before she started to shock her. On the day, Amirah decided to start using the collar, Frankie walked toward the garbage. Once Frankie placed her two paws on the plastic garbage can, Amirah gave the warning and then a shock. Frankie moved her head a bit, but continued to go into the garbage. Cautiously, because Amirah didn't want to hurt Frankie, she gave the dog another warning and then a shock. This time Frankie barely moved.

Once Amirah got Frankie away from the garbage using her old tricks, she brought her dog in and adjusted to e-collar settings to a little higher shock. Later that night, Frankie got back into the garbage. Amirah gave her a warning and then shock, causing Frankie to jump back from the garbage.

When Amirah and Frankie came in, she told her husband what happened. They immediately called friends who use e-collars on their dogs and told them about it. "I would say that the level might be too strong for Frankie. She notices the shock at the first level you had her at, so I would move it back down. It sounds like you will need to give her the warning and shock before she gets to the garbage. Her mission isn't the garbage can, it is what is inside of the garbage can. Therefore, I don't think she will become frightened or aggressive toward garbage cans if she gets near one. Once she gets into the garbage, she is too interested in the garbage to care too much about the shock. Black labs are hunters and very determined dogs, it is hard to remove them from anything they set their minds on.

Amirah followed her friend's advice and noticed it helped. Within a couple of weeks, Frankie would walk toward the garbage, but then hesitate. The moment she started to hesitate, Amirah watched her dog closely. If Frankie took another step closer to the garbage, she gave the warning. If Frankie walked away, nothing happened. The dog wouldn't hear the warning sound. Soon, Frankie didn't worry about the garbage by the side of the garage.

Chapter 4

What You Need to Know Before Training Begins

Before you start training, you might feel overwhelmed about training your companion. At this point, it is important to remember that your dog and can sense your emotions. Therefore, if you are feeling anxious, they are going to start to feel the same way. They will associate their anxious feeling with training. This will interfere with their training and make their experience harder on you and your dog.

General Training Tips for Dogs at Any Age

There are tons of tips that you can use when training your dog. The most important factor to remember is you need to work with your dog. You need to do what is best for yourself and your dog. If you don't work together, the training system can easily fall apart. Below are several other training tips to help you and your dog thrive through the training experience.

Know Your House Rules

It's important that you don't just come up with a rule on the whim. Before you bring your puppy home and start to train, you need to make sure you know your house rules. You can do this by asking yourself basic questions. Do you want your dog laying on the couch? Are you going to let them freely eat or will you only feed them during certain times of the day? Are they going to have one area of the home they can stay in, run around the home, or will your dog remain outside?

Think about your dog's safety around your home. If you are getting a puppy, they can get into everything like toddlers do. It never hurts to ensure they can't open your cupboards with the cleaning products or get into your garbage.

No matter how hard you try, you won't come up with every single house rule right away. There are a lot of rules that you will think of once your dog comes into your home. For example, you might feel it's not okay to let them sleep with you on the bed, but have a change of heart once you bring them home. This is fine, I have done this myself, the key is you need to be consistent with your house rules. Don't change them once you have started training your dog because you "give up" on training or are "too tired to care." Inconsistency is going to confuse your dog and start to destroy trust.

Always Be Consistent

Consistency is one of the most important steps when you are training your dog. Consistency is one of the best ways they will learn. Furthermore, they will learn quickly, trust you, and know good vs bad behavior. Your dog wants to please you. Nearly every breed works on pleasing their owners. They don't want to do something wrong, but it is going to happen. It happens to everyone –human and animal–and is a part of the learning process. The more consistent you are, the easier your dog will adjust to their new home and rules.

Unfortunately, people struggle with consistency for many reasons. For example, you aren't home during the day, meaning you don't know what your dog does. When you come home and find they got into the garbage or tore up the pillow, you can't get after them at that moment because they won't understand. You always need to catch your animals in the act when teaching them what is right and wrong.

Some people aren't consistent because they have busy days and are tired when they come home. They tend to become relaxed with their dogs and let them do what they want because they don't want to train their companions. While I do understand how tired one can get at the end of the day, it is essential that you don't let yourself fall into this thinking trap. That's all it is–a thinking trap. When you decide to bring home a dog and train them, it is your responsibility to keep up on this training, no matter how tired you are. Don't relax on your training because the one who is going to suffer from that is your dog.

Here are some tips to help you focus on consistency in your training:

1. Keep your daily routines. Set a schedule before you bring your new family member home and stick to it as much as possible. Of course, you will have emergency situations and something might change here and there. But, the more consistent you are with the schedule, the easier consistency is with training. Another reason to keep your daily routine is because it teaches the dog that these are normal parts of their day. Have you ever taken a minute to think about how stressful life can be for a dog? They have a lot of situations that can cause them anxiety, such as walking in busy traffic or being home alone for eight hours a day. A routine will help your dog feel more comfortable about their day.

2. Be consistent with your cues. Your dog is about to get into the garbage can on Sunday morning, so you say in a stern voice, "No." Your dog backs away and goes to play. The next morning, your dog is going to do the same thing and you tell them, "No no" in a lighter voice. Your dog continues to go toward the garbage, which is when you say more firmly "No," and your dog backs away. The problem with this

example is you are not consistent. If you say "no" in a firm voice once, you need to do that every time. Don't add another "no" or change your tone of voice as this will confuse your dog, which is why they kept going toward the garbage. The same goes with any nonverbal cues.
3. Keep your words simple. If you are training your dog to come to you by saying the following phrases, "come here," "come," and "come now," you are confusing your dog because they don't mean the same thing. Dogs listen to every word you tell them, and they will understand something different when they hear "here" and "now." Therefore, if you want your dog to come to you, simply use the word "come."
4. Don't do all your daily training at once. Training your dog for 20 minutes in one segment can become too much. They aren't going to remember everything, they will become confused, and they are going to get tired and annoyed. Your dog's attention span is similar to a toddlers–it is very short. The best option is to do any type of training in 2 - 3 minutes segments throughout the day.
5. Everyone needs to be on the same page. This can get a bit challenging if you have younger children who want to train, but everyone in the household should understand the house rules and train the dog in the same way. This can also be a challenge when you have company over. For example, you are training your dog not to jump on people, but your friend rewards the dog with petting and acting excited when your dog jumps on them. This will cause your training to take a step back. It is up to you to explain your training to your friend so they can help your dog understand that jumping on people is not acceptable. With everyone, including guests, being on the same page, your dog will quickly learn the house rules and stick with them.

Stay Healthy

Training is stressful, for both you and your dog. One of the best ways to give yourself the energy to train and keep your mind clear is to stay healthy. At the same time, you need to keep your dog healthy so they will have the best training experiences.

Making sure both you and your dog eat healthy is a great start to staying healthy. For dogs, you need to buy food for them that is nutritious, meaning you want to stick to their diet that is natural for them. This food will be a little more expensive than other food, but it will keep your dog healthy and strong. You want food that has a lot of protein, calcium, active enzymes, essential amino acids, and fatty acids. With these nutrients, your dog is more alert and pay more attention to what you are saying, your tone of voice, and your actions.

One factor you need to keep in mind with your dog's diet is transitioning. If you find you aren't feeding them the best balanced diet and find a different blend of food, such as Primal, you want to transition them to the new food. You want to start things off slow and steady, especially in the first week.

For the first two to three days, mix their regular food with the new food. At this point, you will have about ¾ their old food and ¼ cup Primal food. Watch your dog when they are eating to see how they react to the Primal food. If there are no problems and they eat it, add more Primal food and less old food on the fourth day by giving ½ old food and ½ Primal food.

It is possible that your dog can start having some bowel stress or gastrointestinal problems. When this happens, simply add one tablespoon of Goat Milk to their meal. Mix it well to ensure they get all the Goat Milk possible.

Once the seventh day rolls around, you can decrease the amount of old food to ¼ and increase the Primal formula to ¾. Then, on day ten, you will stop giving your dog any of their old and food strictly give them Primal food. While their system should be used to the Primal formula, it's always a good idea to monitor your dog's bowel movements for a few more days.

While you are working on your dog's diet, you can switch your diet as well. For instance, you might cut out sugars or eat food higher in healthy fats and lower in carbohydrates. Just like you do for your dog, introduce your new diet slowly and you will find that by day ten, both you and your dog are more alert and ready for the best training experience possible.

Getting enough sleep is another factor in staying healthy. It isn't always easy to make sure your dog gets the sleep they need, but they tend to do this pretty well. If you notice your dog struggling to sleep in their bed or in the area they are supposed to sleep in, do a little research to find out why. Another sign that your dog isn't sleeping well is they will find a different spot to sleep instead of lay in their bed. If you find your dog in a certain spot every morning, allow them to fall asleep in this spot and see if they remain their all night. Dogs will naturally get up throughout the night to stretch, check on you, or get some water. However, if they have a comfortable place to sleep, they will go straight back into that location until their day is supposed to start.

Be Patient

It is going to take time to train your dog and if they came from a shelter or have previous bad experiences, it will be harder. Dogs who come from abusive situations or are abandoned fear that these experiences are going to happen again. Like humans, they don't want to go through the physical and emotional pain it causes them. They want to feel loved in secure in their new home, but it is hard for them to trust you.

The best key to help your dog heal from any previous trauma is to be patient. Understand that your dog is emotionally and mentally hurting and you need to maintain a calm and trusting environment to help them through their emotions.

You also need to understand that some dogs will always have emotional and mental scars from previous trauma. They are similar to humans in this way, but aren't able to work through their emotions and mental scarring through therapy like humans can.

If you know or believe that your new family member was abused, here are some helpful tips to help your dog overcome their internal battles.

1. Get down to their level. Don't stand up and talk to your dog if they are afraid as this will make them feel inferior and increase their fear of you. Getting down to their level makes them feel equal to you.
2. Off them a treat. This isn't something everyone will do, but treats always make dogs feel better. Think about how often you want to have a treat after a bad day. Dogs feel the same way. Plus, giving them a treat reminds them that you love and care about them, immediately improving their mental state.
3. Make sure your dog has a safe place. You will start to know when your dog is uncomfortable or afraid through their reactions. When you notice your dog showing signs of this behavior, bring them to a secure place. This could be their area in the house, garage, or any place they feel the most comfortable. If you aren't in their secure place at home, take them out of the environment and spend quality time with them.
4. Don't forget about a pet behaviorist. It's important that you don't give up on your dog. Doing this will only increase their emotional and psychological trauma. If you find that you are having trouble handling your pet's behavior because of their past abuse or abandonment, bring them to a pet behaviorist. They will help you understand where your pet is coming from and give you ideas on how to help your pet overcome their trauma.

Reward Good Behavior

As a trainer, you don't want to get in the habit of shocking your dog with unwanted behavior. For success, you need to reward good behavior, including when your dog backs away from the unwanted behavior. For example, you are outside and training your dog not to go into the chicken coop. You have a curious puppy, and they often find the noises coming from the chicken coop interesting. Every time they pass the gate into the chicken coop, you give your dog a warning before a shock. Each time you see your dog, you ask them to "come" and wave your hand. They follow this direction and you give them a treat for coming to you when you called.
If you are training your dog and know you will need to give them a lot of treats, don't focus on unhealthy or bigger treats. Get some healthy treats that will help boost your dog and not drag him down. Too many unhealthy treats can cause stomach issues and make your dog sick. It's also possible to give him a little piece of a bigger healthy treat each time he follows your direction while training.

Obedience Classes

No matter what age your dog is, you can always enroll them in an obedience class. In fact, this is a great way to make certain your dog is socializing and you are receiving the right help you need for training. There is a lot of information that goes into training, and it is difficult to simply start training your dog without research and advice.
There are some dog owners who feel they don't need to spend the money on obedience training because their dog is "good enough." While you have a great dog, there are many benefits that are included in obedience training.
   1. You will meet like-minded dog owners. While you may have friends with dogs, this doesn't mean that take training as seriously as you do. When you take your dog to an obedience school, you will meet people who have some of the same ideas and goals for their dog that you do. You will find someone who can help you through the training process or

find someone to talk to about you and your dog's failures and successes with training.
2. You will expand your knowledge. No matter how much research you do on training, obedience classes will expand your knowledge further. Your dog isn't the only one who will learn from the class.
3. You will build your bond with your dog. One of the best steps of obedience school is building your connection to your dog. This is a special time for you and your dog, and you will both feel it. Your dog will feel that you care about their general well-being and you will feel like you are doing everything you can to ensure your dog has a great training experience.

What Happens in Obedience Classes?

Sometimes dog owners are weary about obedience classes because they feel only dogs with behavioral problems go to them. This is a myth as any dog at any age will benefit from an obedience class. Furthermore, any dog owner will benefit from a class.
Another reason dog owners are cautious about obedience classes is they don't understand what happens in them. They feel it is simply teaching your dog tricks, but this is only a part of it. Obedience classes help your dog to understand what their role is with you and within the world. They will not only learn the basic commands, but also social skills. You will begin to understand healthy behaviors from negative behaviors when it comes to your dog. In general, you will feel closer to your companion because you will understand what they are telling you when they act a certain way.

Your Dog's Age Matters

The age of your dog matters when you are trying to train them. While dogs can be trained at any age, it is a lot easier to train puppies than older dogs. Some people feel they have to get a puppy if they want to train a dog, yet don't have the energy or ability to take care of an energetic puppy. Fortunately, this is a myth and senior dogs can learn just as well as puppies.

When it comes down to the basics, a senior dog is going to learn just like a puppy. However, a senior dog may take more time to learn the tricks than puppies. Part of this is because a senior dog is set in their ways, just like human adults get set in their ways. Another part is because senior dogs are generally slower. They are going to take more time to reach their paw up to shake or lay down. As long as you are patient and consistent, you will find your training fits with dogs of any age.

If you recently got an older dog from a shelter, get whatever information you can about their background as this will help you understand how your dog is going to react to training. Another reason is because you want to try to learn what tricks older dogs already know. For example, were they taught to sit by the previous owner and how? While this might be impossible to learn, you can work with your dog, a pet behaviorist, and a trainer to get an idea of how they were trained. You can start by telling the dog to sit–if they sit repeatedly at this command, they understand. If they don't sit continuously, they may have received inconsistent training.

For older dogs, you need to understand if they have physical disabilities that will stop them from doing certain tricks. First, you should never train a senior dog to do highly active tricks, such as learning how to surf or riding a skateboard. Senior dogs don't have the same strong bones as puppies and can get hurt easily. A veterinarian will tell you if your new dog has any type of disabilities and what they can learn vs what is too much for them.

Before you take in an older dog, you need to make certain you are ready for the responsibility. A lot of people think puppies take more responsibility, but in reality, senior dogs can because of any health problems. For example, taking in a blind dog with arthritis means medication and a lot of trips to the veterinarian's office. You will also need to care for the dog just as much as a puppy. For example, a blind dog will need to be slowly taken around their environment, so they don't constantly run into things. They will usually walk slower and be more cautious because they are afraid of running into something.

Case Example: Alice the Trainer and Her Dogs

I have raised many dogs throughout my life. My father bought my first dog, a Pitbull puppy, when I was eight years old. I named him Jake, and he taught me a lot about responsibility. When I was 15 years old, my parents allowed me to take in another puppy, a Black Lab named Buddy. To see the difference between Jack and Buddy amazed me. I knew that Buddy would be more energetic, but I never thought that Jack would become exhausted from Buddy. He really couldn't keep up with the puppy, no matter how hard he tried.

At one point, I noticed that Buddy wouldn't leave Jack alone. Even when Jack tried to go off to be alone and rest, Buddy tried to get him to play more or to get his attention in other ways. I quickly realized I needed to train Buddy not to bother Jack when he needed a break. At first, I thought of putting Buddy's e-collar on and shocking him when he would walk near Jack as he tried to rest. But I worried that this could cause Buddy to not want to play with Jack at all. Therefore, I started to train Buddy through a reward system. I didn't give him treats because I didn't want Jack to feel left out with the treats, but I would bring Buddy into another room and play with him or give him a treat without Jack knowing. Slowly, Buddy started to go to Jack when he went to lay down, sniff him, and then walk away.

This experience helped me realize the difference between young and old dogs, and I soon found myself focusing on professional training. Over the past 20 years, I have trained over 200 dogs of all ages. One of the first topics I discuss with all my clients is how the age of the dog matters when it comes to training, but only to a point. You can train older dogs, just like younger dogs, but you have to make sure older dogs get more breaks. They are going to get tired quickly. They are slower, but also determined to make your proud. They need the same consistency, patience, and care with their training that a puppy needs.

Training Your Puppy

Training a puppy is a fun, enjoyable, and stressful experience. While you enjoy seeing them learn and grow, they can also keep you on your toes. They don't have a strong attention span and can easily become distracted. However, they also want to do everything they can to please you, even the more stubborn breeds. Here are a few tips when it comes to training your puppy.

Your Puppy is Not an Infant and Not an Adult

Puppies are at a bit of an in-between age when it comes to the life of dogs. They are still growing and developing on a physical, mental, and emotional level. Yet, they are not infant dogs and can do more than you think by themselves. Because of their age, people struggle to know the best way to train their puppy. I know many trainers who have helped people through the difficulties of training a puppy.

Your Puppy's Developmental Stages

There are several developmental stages that your puppy is going to go through before they reach adulthood. You want to understand these stages so you can get the best out of them when it comes to training.

At four weeks, you should get your puppy socializing with other dogs. If you are a breeder or your dog had puppies, you shouldn't give them away until they are a little over eight weeks old. There is a lot of development that goes on within this time and allowing them to play with their brothers, sisters, and parents will help them grow mentally, physically, and emotionally.

Starting at five weeks old, they should interact more with humans. Of course, if you have children they are going to want to play with the puppies immediately. Try to hold off on letting them around the puppies too much until about week five.

At five weeks old, they will also start to become little investigators. They will get into everything they can and become interested in their environment. Let the roam around as much as possible, but also keep your eye on them. Puppies at this age can fit into the smallest places, causing them to get stuck.

Puppies need the first few weeks of their life to develop their dog-to-dog training skills. This is something you should not interrupt. By week eight, they will have developed more of their primary dog skills and might be ready for a new home. If you bring a puppy home around week eight, continue to focus on their social skills. Don't worry about full-on training yet and do not prepare an e-collar for your dog. Any dog should be at least six months old before you start thinking about an e-collar

By ten weeks, you want to make sure your puppy has had plenty of socializing opportunities and explored their surroundings. If they haven't they will start to become easily afraid of the unfamiliar. This is an anxiety that the dog will carry with them throughout their life, making them more difficult to train.

A Puppy's Fears

Before you start training, you have to understand your puppy's personality, including their fears. Most puppies are going to have some type of fears, especially in a new home. First, if you notice your puppy acting startled when they come across something or a person they don't recognize, this is natural. They will recover easily and try to see what this new stimuli is all about. They will continue to be curious and eventually grow out of the startling phase. However, all dogs will naturally be a little hesitant when it comes to new stimuli.

The trouble with puppies and their fears is if they don't show signs of recovery after a few minutes. There are many warning signs that will alert you to their fear:

- Trembling
- Scanning the room
- Lack bladder or bowel control
- They want to withdraw from the environment
- Whining
- They are trying to avoid what is scaring them
- Excessive panting
- Refusing to eat
- Vomiting
- Diarrhea
- Salivating

If your puppy starts showing some of these signs, of course they won't be potty trained yet, around five weeks old, they may have inherited fearful tendencies from a parent. At three months old, your dog will start to become anxious if you don't do what you can to help them through their intense fear. Once a dog becomes anxious, they will remain this way for the rest of their life.

Don't Start House Training Until Eight Weeks Old

While you shouldn't worry about an e-collar at this point, you can start basic training with your dog at eight weeks old. One of the first steps you will do is train them on their main spot. This is the area where they will eat, sleep, and spend the majority of their time. For example, if they will be an inside dog, they will remain indoors. If they are outside dogs, they go outside the majority of the time. It is essential that you teach them their potty spot at this age.

Training a Puppy Takes a Certain Mindset

Justin opened his own dog training business 25 years ago. The mission of his business is not just to help people learn how to train their dogs with an e-collar, but to overcome the challenges of training. "A lot of people tend to give up because they feel some forms of training are a lost cause. If they can't give their puppy to stop jumping on people, they become more relaxed about it because it's not worth the struggle. I have had people tell me they have other things to worry about than getting their dog to listen to them about everything. This is the wrong mindset to have when it comes to training. I always tell people who say something like this that they need to develop a more compassionate and tougher mindset. They need the compassion so their dog still feels comfortable around them. Compassion can also help them understand their dog needs consistency in training. A tougher mindset is more for them than their dog. This mindset doesn't allow you to give up. You want to remain strong because you want to do the best for your dog."

Training Your Older Dog

While most training tips are pretty general between puppies and older dogs, there are a few factors that are more important for older dogs.

You Can Train Them for a Longer Period of Time

Older dogs have a longer attention span than puppies. While you should start with shorter training sessions, such as 10 to 20 minutes twice a day, you can increase this amount of time little by little. For example, if you start with 10 minutes, two weeks in you can increase to 12 minutes. Always watch your dog and notice if they start to get distracted or too tired. You don't want to force them to go longer than they can handle.
Always remember, each breed is different. Some breeds are going to naturally have longer attention spans than other breeds. For example, Border Collies, Labradors, and German Shepherds have some of the longest attention spans because they have high levels of concentration.

You Need More Patience

You always need patience when training your furry friend, but you need more patience with older dogs. You can teach an old dog new tricks, but it is going to take longer than it will for a puppy. Puppies naturally catch onto new tricks quicker because of their age and curiosity level. Older dogs are not as curious, and like people, tend to slow down.
It's natural to feel like giving up on your training sometimes, you might even feel this way with a puppy. The key is to take a break if you need to–your dog might need a break too. Take a few deep breaths and think about all the process you and your dog have made. Sometimes people look so far into how much work they need to do that they forget about their progress. Don't let this happen to you as it will make you feel like training isn't working.

Socialize Your Dog

Just like puppies need socializing, adult dogs need to socialize just as well. No matter what age your dog is, they need to run, play, meet with other dogs, and people. Otherwise, dogs can suffer from fear, shyness, and loneliness. They won't know how to interact with people or other dogs. Other than the park or having your dog meet your friends and family, take them on walks with other dogs and dog training classes.

Get to Know Your Dog

If you don't know about your adult dog's past, take them to a dog behaviorist and a trainer. They can help you learn to understand your dog's past a little better by the way they act. Training dogs is always easier when you can understand certain behaviors.

Chapter 5

Let the Training Begin

Tips to Prepare Your Dog for Training

While I've already discussed several tips to prepare your dog for training, I want to bring up a few more. Some of these tips will focus on home training and some on obedience training.

Always Have Your Dog's Attention Prior to Training

E-collar training is not going to work if you don't have your dog's attention. When you first use the e-collar, you need a way to grab your dog's attention when you are going to give them a command. You might do this by tugging on their leash if you are outdoors or saying their name. You might decide to use some kind of motion, such as snapping your fingers twice. Once you can consistently gain your dog's attention, you can start with basic training.

Make Sure You Have a Little Play Time

If your dog is too energetic to focus on training, the whole process is going to fail. Play with your dog before you start training. You can take them for a walk or to the park. Do something that is outdoors as this will calm your dog out more than playing inside. Don't give them too much exercise because you don't want to make them too tired for training. The point is to let them run off enough energy so they feel calm and can focus on their training.

Have Everything You Need with You

You want all your training supplies right next to you when you start training. If you have to head to grab the treat, your dog is going to get distracted and then you need to start over. Place the treats in your pocket or hide them in some way so your dog doesn't notice them and focus on the treats instead of training. If you are going to implement the e-collar, have this available to you, if it's not already on your dog's neck. You can even have a few toys near you to reward your dog by playing with them for a while when they follow through with your command.

Empty Your Dog's Stomach

Don't feed your dog right before you are going to train them or head to a training session. If they need to use the bathroom, they will become distracted or could have an accident. While accidents can still happen, feeding your dog a few hours before you start training will help avoid accidents.

Every Dog Should Know the Basic Commands

There are a lot of tricks that you can teach your dog. You can teach them the basic commands or you can become more advanced. In general, what you decide to teach your dog is up to you and your dog. While every dog, no matter what age, should know the basic commands such as stay, sit and lay down, not every dog will want to learn other tricks. For example, your older dog shouldn't learn how to ride a skateboard. You don't need to train your dogs to jump rope, hide their head, wave, shake hands, or hug. You might feel these are fun tricks, but if your dog isn't into it, they shouldn't be forced.

Basic Commands

Finally, after all the information you've received it is finally time to start looking at some basic training strategies. The training techniques you will learn in this chapter don't all need an e-collar. While it is your choice to use an e-collar to teach your dog to sit or not, some professional trainers advise against it while others say it works great for basic training.

Some of the basic training techniques are best used with a reward system instead of a shock if your dog doesn't listen to your commands. However, if you struggle with training and feel you and your dog will benefit from the e-collar, then it is up to you. All you need to do is make sure your dog can handle the e-collar. For example, if your puppy is only four months old, even the smaller e-collars might be too much, but you can still try. You also need to remember to follow your dog. They will let you know if something is too much for them.

Bed Training

Some people feel that the e-collar should not be used for bed training. Like any training you do with the e-collar, it is generally up to you. If you feel you and your dog are ready for the e-collar, then use it for this type of training. You can also use this training to teach them to go into their create.

Step One: Facing the Bed

When you start this training, you want them to face their bed. Point to their bed and say "bed" and give a tone. Once your dog is all the way in their bed, turn your e-collar off. You should never have the e-collar on when they are sleeping. Always remember to praise your dog when they do something they should.

Your dog is going to be confused about the "bed" command at first; this is common when you just start training them in a new task. Don't spend too much time on forcing them to go to bed and don't stress them out by pushing the stimulation button over and over. You also need to be careful about disciplining your dog if they don't listen because they can associate this with bed. At the same time, if you give up you are telling your dog they have options and that's not building a strong training foundation.

You know your dog the best and you will probably come up with a solution to help your dog understand that the word "bed" means lay down and go to sleep. For example, you might find that putting a treat in their bed helps then understand or using hand gestures. Whatever extra training tool you use, you need to slowly reverse the action because you want them to go to bed when you give the command of "bed."

Step Two: Back Farther Away From the Bed

Once your dog is going to bed easily when you stand right next to his bed, you want to back up a bit. You can go into the next room and repeat the command. By this time, your dog will understand what "bed" and the tone means. They will more than likely head straight to their bed because you asked them to and they want the tone to stop. Dogs are great at figuring out how to get things to stop as they know what is in their best interest. Therefore, your dog is going to head to his bed because he hears the tone and the only way to get the tone to stop is by laying down in bed.

You can continue to back farther away from the bed as much as you want. For instance, if you allow your dog to roam all over the house, you never really know where you will be when you need to tell them "bed." Dogs tend to remember the scenery they are trained in and will associate this with the command. This does mean that your dog will understand the word "bed" and know what it means when you say it in the living room, but if you have never said it in this room before, they might not go right away.

Home Base and Perimeter Training

Every dog owner has the fear of their dog running off. Some people fear this so much that they don't let their dog outside unless they are with them and their dog is on a leash. Other people are a little more relaxed and will simply hope their dog stays within the yard.
One of the first basic training strategies that you need to teach your dog is their home base, sometimes called perimeter training. This is when you tell a dog where they sleep, where they can go in your house, where they can't go, where they will go potty, eat, etc. Dogs are not a companion you can walk around the house and say, "You go potty here, you go to bed here, you can't go in this room" and expect them to know. They have to be trained, and it will take time.
This training won't keep them at home. Your dog is going to run if they want and can run. The main point of this training is to help them understand what their role is in the home. It also establishes the owner/dog relationship.

Step One: What Are Your Dog's Boundaries?

To teach your dog where they can go and can't, you need to make sure you set up boundaries before training and stick to them. For example, your dog can go in the living room, but not on the furniture. They can't go into the kitchen, but can stay in the porch, walk-in coat closet, and entry way. You also decide your dog can go to the basement, but not into bedrooms.
You want to do the same thing with your yard. If you live in town, but don't have a fence, you will want to think about how to keep your dog within your yard. This might be difficult with a leash, but it is possible to do your best in training your dog not to leave your yard.

Step Two: Establish Home Base with Your Dog

Before you use the e-collar for home base training, you need to make sure your dog understands the type of training you will work on. You can do this by verbally telling them and spend a few days or a couple of weeks allowing your dog to become comfortable in the home, at least in the areas they are allowed in.
If you have used the e-collar before, you will understand that you want to get your dog comfortable before using. If you haven't used e-collar training previously, follow the steps in Chapter 2 when getting your dog used to home base training.

Step Three: Mark the Boundaries with Cones, Flags, or Anything Noticeable to a Dog

Your dog isn't going to understand the boundaries unless they are clearly marked. If you don't have a fence, sidewalk, or anything else to mark your dog's boundaries outside, you want to think of using cones or flags. You can then teach them that any place beyond the flag or cone is too far.

Step Four: Walk Your Dog to Their Home Base

No matter where the home base is, take your dog's leash and walk them to their home base. Once they are in the area, give them a treat. You will want to do this a few times throughout a series of days. Don't take 10 to 15 minutes and walk them to and from their home base and this may confuse them or stress them out. Plus, it would give them too many treats and they will become sick. Instead, take a couple of minutes to do this about two to three times a day.

Step Five: Reinforce with Verbal Commands

Some people will combine this step with step four right away. It is up to you to do this. I don't do this because I feel separating them gives your dog more time to understand their training. Remember, you need to have patience when you are training your dog.

You want to keep the commands short. For example, you might say "home" to let them know to go to their home base. If you have their bed at their home base, which is typically the case, you can say "bed." You probably won't want to use the verbal cue for "lay" or "lay down" as this should be saved for when you want to train your dog to lie down and relax around company or in another setting. Other words they will want to recognize when it comes to their home base is "stop" and "come." You will use stop when you don't want them to go any farther and come when you want them to come back.
Some people will also use a hand gesture during this phase. They may point to their dog's home base or move their hand in that direction. The biggest problem with using hand gestures is you can use the same gesture throughout your day and not notice. This will confuse your dog when you are sending them to their home base or trying to tell someone which direction to go.

Step Six: Repetitive Training

In this step, you will focus on perimeter training. This is when you look at the whole area your dog can go to and not just where their bed, food, or water is. When you are focusing on perimeter training, you want to make a distinction between home base and the rest of the boundaries. For instance, you will tell them to go "home," meaning home base, when you want them to go to bed or lay down. You will then walk them around the perimeter. You can allow them to walk freely as this will give you time to tell them "stop" or "come" when they go too far.
This step is going to take a while. You will want to spend at least a week, if not more, focusing on this step. Don't take your dog around too often when you are working on this step. While you want to repeat it for a while, you don't want to spend too much time training your dog where they can go and where they can't go. For a puppy, you should keep all training times to two to three minutes, an adult dog at about five minutes, and a senior dog can handle about 10 minutes.
At this point, you should only use the e-collar if you feel your dog is ready for it. Because this is still a basic training step, though at a deeper level, you don't need to use the e-collar yet.

Step Seven: Introduce the E-Collar

If you haven't done so yet, now is the best time to train your dog on their perimeter training with the e-collar. You want to ensure that they understand their training and are grasping the concept. You also want to make sure that you follow the right steps when introducing the e-collar.

Step Eight: Go Beyond the Perimeter

This next step is debatable for many dog owners as they feel it is a trick more than a test. In this step, you want to test your dog to make sure they do not follow you beyond the boundaries. Why many dog owners have problems with this step is because you need to ask your dog to "come" to you when you are outside of their boundaries.

The point of this step is to make sure they understand the importance of remaining in their boundaries. Another reason is because it helps set up the owner/dog relationship where you give them rules and they follow. When you use the e-collar, you will give them a warning and shock them if they pass beyond their boundaries. Of course, you can always use your verbal cues if you don't feel right testing your dog with the e-collar. Other people won't use the e-collar until they have reached this stage and their dog stays within the boundaries. It's always important to remember that dog training is a little flexible when it comes to you and your dog. You need to figure out what works for you and not what other people say.

Step Nine: Reinforcement Phase

In this step, you will allow your dog to freely move around the perimeter and remain hidden from their sight. However, you want to see where your dog is going. The reason why you want to watch is your dog is so you can give them a warning and shock if they cross the boundary. They won't know it is you and will think it is because they are going farther than the flags or cones allow them to.

You can also use this phase to test what your dog will do if something distracts them. For example, if they are outside, will they run toward a passing car? Of course, you will use your training method to bring them back into their perimeter. If they do become distracted, you know that you have more training to go before you can officially wean them off the e-collar for this training.

Sit Training

Whenever you start a new training technique, you want them to be in their home base area.

Step One: Say the Command

Use your attention grabbing technique to get your dog's attention. Say "sit" once with any hand gesture you are going to use to motion them to sit. This gesture needs to be different than the one you will use to tell them to lay down. When you get them to sit, reward them.

Step Two: Add in the E-collar

When you are training your dog, you can start using the e-collar right away, like we did with bed training, or you can wait until they understand the command. In this training technique, I am adding the e-collar in a bit later to show you how it works and why. You want your dog to understand their new command. You can make them feel stressed if you use the e-collar and they don't understand what they are supposed to do. This is going to get training off to a bad start and make you and your dog become too dependent on the e-collar.

When you add in the e-collar in the middle of training, you want the e-collar to replace your old techniques, such as a hand gesture or a treat. Your dog won't understand the change immediately, so you will want to use both techniques at the same time while slowly decreasing your old technique. For example, the first couple of commands with the e-collar, you will use both techniques. Then, when you feel your dog understands the tone or vibration of their e-collar with the command, you will stop using the other technique. If your dog responds, continue using only the e-collar. If your dog doesn't respond like they were, continue using your old technique at least two more times before repeating this process.

Once you say "sit" send the tone to the e-collar to get your dog associated with the tone (or vibration) and command. Remember to reward them if they sit. Your dog is going to make a mistake a few times and not sit when they are told to. This is normal for dogs, especially puppies, because they are easily distracted and still learning. Even if your dog doesn't listen to the command right away, when they do, follow it with positive reinforcement. Dogs thrive on positive reinforcement, and it will help them learn the command and want to perform.

Step Three: Practice

Just like you did with bed training, practice telling your dog to "sit" in various locations. You can even take them outside of the house to practice as you will have moments of telling your dog to sit wherever you go, such as a friend's house. The key when you practice is to not focus on the task too long and to remain consistent in your methods as much as possible. For instance, there might be times where you don't have the e-collar on and you need to tell your dog to sit.

Lay Down Training

Step One: Home Base

You need to make sure that your dog is in their home base area before you start the training. This is a consistent step whenever you start a new training method as it helps them learn. Plus, they are most comfortable in their home base environment. When your dog follows you into their home base environment, you will reward them. This is always an important step when it comes to your dog successfully completing any step in training.

Step Two: Say the Command

Tell your dog to "lay down." You don't want them to go to bed and lay down because this is going to confuse your dog with the "bed" and "lay down" command. You want to make sure that these two commands are separate and your dog understands this.
When you tell your dog to "lay down" you want to make sure you have their attention and you use a hand gesture or another type of technique they are used to in training. While you can start with the e-collar right way, like we did with the bed training, you can also wait to include the e-collar in the next step.

Step Three: Add in the E-Collar

This step follows the same format that telling your dog to sit does. You will add in the e-collar and turn it on right before you give the dog your command. Remember to reinforce the command with your previous gestures so they understand that the stimulation they feel is telling them to lie down. Again, even if your dog makes a few mistakes along the way, ensure that you always give them positive reinforcement when they follow the command.

Step Four: Practice

Once you are just using the e-collar to reinforce the command, start to practice in various areas around your home, outside, and even at a friend's house. Just as you did with teaching your dog to sit, you will use this command in various locations.

Another factor to remember when teaching your dog to lay down is that they will often follow commands and then get up back and want to play, especially puppies. You may have noticed this when you taught your dog to sit. It's important, especially with lay down, that the dog remains in that position for a few seconds, at least. You might want to train them to stay that way for a few minutes, but you always need to gradually train your dog. At the same time, you don't want to force your dog to lie down for too long, no matter where you are. This can cause them to become stressed, especially if they are energetic dogs. You should always think about your dog's personality when you are training them. This will help you ensure that you and your dog have the best training experience possible.

Come Training

Many people feel it is also important that you train your dog to "come" after you have trained them to "sit." This is because it will give them a sense of freedom from their last command. While some dogs might sit and then get up right away, especially if they notice you have a treat or toy in your hand, other dogs will sit for a period of time or until you ask move or train them to come to you.

Step One: Home Base

You always want to start training your dog at their home base no matter what you are trying to teach them. Most trainers feel that starting at the dog's home base is essential for this training.

Before you start training, choose a spot to stand within their home base. This spot is the area they will come to. If you move around too much during the first few times of the training, you will confuse your dog. They won't understand exactly where they are supposed to go when you say "come." You will focus on moving around later in the training.

Step Two: Say the Command

Following the same method you did with "sit" and "lay down," you will ask your dog to "come" while using a hand gesture or another method of training method they are used to. If you're comfortable starting training with the e-collar, it's fine to include it in this step.

There is a chance that your dog is going to come to you before you even give the command. They don't understand what is going on, so they are going to question why you are standing away from them. This is especially true for a puppy. Bring them back toward their bed or a bit away from you and try again.

When your dog performs the command, give them positive reinforcement. This doesn't always have to be a treat. Dogs love any type of positive reinforcement, including special attention and play time.

If you haven't used the e-collar to help reinforce this training yet, you should do so once your dog has performed the action a few times.

Step Three: Follow-up with an Additional Command

This command can easily make your dog wander, causing them to become confused. They may not understand when the command is done and continue to follow you. Because you always want to make sure your dog understands that the command is over, you can follow-up with another command. You can use any other trick that your dog knows, but most people use the "sit" command.

People will often use "sit" "lay down" and "come" training together. For example, you might ask your dog to "sit" before requesting them to "lay down." This is helpful for a dog because it gives them one step at a time. Some trainers will command their dog to do all three in a row. Of course, you want to do this slowly and make sure you are telling them on type of training at the time. For instance you will tell them to "sit" and then let them sit for a few seconds before commanding them to "lay down." Once they are down for a few seconds, you then command them to "come."

If you do this as practice, you want to make sure you don't place stress on your dog by performing the commands over and over within a small amount of time. For example, you don't want to spend a half hour repeatedly telling them to "sit," "lay down," and "come." You want to stick to a session of two to three minutes, no more than five minutes, for puppies and between 10 to 20 minutes for older dogs.

Stay Training

Step One: Home Base

Just like previous training, you want to start at your dog's home base. If they aren't at their home base, ask them to come to the home base. Make sure you give them positive reinforcement for following your command.

Step Two: Say the Command

You will start to teach your dog to stay with a hand gesture and your voice. Using the e-collar right away doesn't always work for this command at first because your dog isn't going to understand that they need to stay in that spot. Furthermore, many dogs will move around when they feel the tone, vibration, or shock from the e-collar. This will only cause problems within your training. You can include the e-collar after your dog understand what they are supposed to do when you say "stay."

Step Three: Reinforce with Another Command

"Stay" is a great command that is used after another command, such as sit or lay down. This is why most trainers believe you should teach your dog to lie down, sit, or come before you teach them to stay. For example, you command your dog to "sit." Once they perform this command, you tell them to "stay." This lets your dog know that they are not supposed to get up until they receive another command from you or they get tired of staying in the spot and want to move around. Always remember that you dog, especially puppies, need to move around regularly. They won't have the patience to stay in one spot for a long time. They need to get up and move.

Get Down Training

This training is a bit different to do because your dog needs to jump on something or someone before you can train them to get down. You can't really predict where this training will take place, so you don't have to bring them into their home base. But, you need to be prepared to start this training at any time.

Some trainers will cause the dog to jump up on something so they can start the training. You can do this if you want to train your dog in their home base, but they can become confused. For example, if they see you place the treats on the table and you allow them to jump up on the table, but then instruct them to get down they are going to receive mixed signals from you.

Step One: Say the Command

After you catch your dog jumping up on something or someone, command them to "get down." Use a hand signal or some other training technique to help them understand the command. You shouldn't use the e-collar at first for this command. They will need to understand what get down means before you use stimulation from the e-collar.

Step Two: Reinforce the Command with the E-Collar

Once your dog successfully follows the "get down" command a couple of times, add in the e-collar to reinforce the training. For instance, you tell your dog to "get down" but they don't listen, so you use the e-collar stimulation to reinforce the training. Like the previous training techniques, you will back away from the hand motion or other type of training reinforcement you used once you start using the e-collar.

Step Three: Everyone Should Positively Reinforce Your Dog

You know how important positive reinforcement is when your dog listens to a command, but the person they jumped on may not. Ask the person to give your dog some positive reinforcement for getting down when you commanded them to. You should explain this to everyone that your dog jumps on.

Chapter 6

Training Strategies, Levels, and Your Dog

By now, you know that your dog's breed and personality sets the tone for training, even with the e-collar. There are several breeds that are difficult to train, such as the Chow Chow, Akita, Siberian Husky, and Chinese Shar-Pei. You can train any breed of dog, but there are some that will give you a harder time than others. It's not because the dogs don't listen, it's typically because they have a hard time socializing or have a stubborn personality.
No matter what breed of dog you have or how old they are, you should always look into obedience school. These schools not only train your dog, but the trainers also help you with any problems you have or understanding training in general. It's another sense of support, especially when you and your furry friend are struggling with training.

Training Levels

Professional trainers of talk about how there are different levels of training. Depending on what trainer you talk to will depend on how many levels they focus on, but in general there are five. These levels might change depending on what school you go to. For example, parts of level one might make their way to level two. Some schools will often combine the first two levels because they are the easiest. This allows the dog trainers to focus more on the two harder levels. While you and your dog will go through these levels in obedience school, you can incorporate them at home as well.

Level One: Foundation Training

The basic training we went through in the previous chapter focused on tricks your dog will learn in level one. This level is meant to teach the dog how to follow commands give them the basics to become a well-mannered companion. As the easiest level, most dog breeds catch on to this information and start to show signs of learning after the first class. Most dog trainers will not focus on the e-collar during level one. However, they may help you learn how to use it or talk about e-collar training at this level. Some schools will have special classes for e-collars at level one. You can always talk to your dog trainer if you are interested in bringing in the e-collar for training at this level.

Level Two: Skill Building Training

If the obedience school separates level one and level two, this level will build off the skills your dog already learned in level one. For example, the only trick you taught your dog in level one was to sit. This is because level two focuses on the exercises you will give your before they start training. A dog trainer in level two may focus on:

- Teaching your dog to "lay down"
- Teaching your dog to "come"
- Teaching your dog to sit whenever you stop walking

Level Three: Reinforce Reliability and Behaviors

By level three, your dog is ready for the more complex tricks. This is usually the level where e-collars are introduced and you can start to bring your dog's e-collar. Most obedience schools will allow you to enroll your dog in special classes, such as therapy dogs, mental exercises, and dog sports.

You and your dog might go through real-life situations where you will need to use basic commands. For example, your dog trainer has you and someone else act like you are walking your dogs down the sidewalk when one of them starts growling at the other. The trainer will then talk to you about how to handle this situation.

Level Four: Advanced Skills

You should understand that your dog doesn't have to take part in all of the levels. In a typical obedience school, you need to enroll your dog in each level. The only factor is you can't enroll your dog into level two without level one. You do have the follow the rules and prerequisites set up by the school.
It's also a good idea to make sure that you celebrate the accomplishments you and your dog have together throughout the training journey. Some people will celebrate with their dog, maybe by getting a special treat after each level. Your dog may not understand what the celebration is all about, but when you are excited your dog is bound to be excited. Furthermore, making it to level four is definitely something for you and your dog to celebrate!
Level four is the time when you start to show off all of the tricks your dog knows. Throughout this level, your dog will refine their skills, so they can amaze people even more with all their knowledge and tricks. At the same time, your dog will learn a few harder tricks or focus on sitting or lying down for a longer period of time. In this level, your dog may learn:
- Waiting at the door. This doesn't necessarily mean your door at home. They will learn to wait at any door. For example, if you head to the store and you can't bring your dog inside, you can leave them outside to wait. Of course, you always want to consider your dog's safety in this case. If you live in a small and rural area, it might be fine, especially if you know and trust everyone. You can also leave your dog in the care of another person you trust while you run into the store. However, if you live in a larger city, it is best not to leave

your dog unattended at all. Many dogs are stolen because they are left unattended in cars or by a store.
- Learning to ignore distractions and follow your commands.
- Walking with you while their leash is loose and ignoring any distractions, such as another dog or people.

Level Five: Expert Training Skills

For most obedience school, this is often the top level. Once you reach this level, your dog has an amazing ability to control their behaviors–most of the time. Remember, your dog is never going to be perfect at training. They will make a mistake from time to time, such as becoming distracted and not listening to your commands. When this happens, it is essential that you use your e-collar as it will motion the dog that this behavior is not acceptable. You should never use the e-collar to discipline your dog because they are not listening. As stated previously, your dog always needs to be exhibiting the unwanted behavior when you use the e-collar. Some of the behaviors your dog will work on during level five are:

- Listening to other people when told to go into a different position, such as when your dog is at the veterinarian's office.
- Staying in the "lay down" or "sit" for a longer period of time
- Sitting until you allow them to move
- Learning when they need to back up so they are not in the way

Practice Real Life Training

Professional trainers will talk to you about practicing real-life training moments before you are surprisingly put on the spot. This will allow you to think through the process you and your dog needs to go through to get the best outcome. When you practice training techniques this way, you can prepare yourself and imagine how you will handle certain situations. For example, if you bring your dog into a store (always make sure the store allows dogs) how will you handle your dog jumping on the shelf and knocking items down? Here are some examples of ways you can practice real-life training. These types of training experiences will work for any breed and dog of any age.

Practice Sitting Politely

One of the first tricks your dog will learn is to sit. One of the easiest training exercises you can bring wherever you go is teaching your dog to sit and wait for your next motion. This is going to be easier for some dogs than others. For example, if you have just started training your puppy, chances are they are not going to sit for a long period. They will sit and then get up a few seconds later. An older dog, especially a senior dog, will sit easier for a period, but it might be a good idea to motion him to lay down eventually. You always want to keep your dog's health in mind when you are training.

Whenever the opportunity arises to get your dog to practice sitting nicely–take it! It's a great way to get your dog used to sitting in various settings. Over time, you will notice him sitting for longer periods of time. This is a great perk about training consistently, your dog is going to adjust and they will find ways to keep themselves occupied when they need to sit or lay down because there is company over. But, no matter how patient your dog becomes, it's important to watch them and notice when they need to get up and move around. If your dog is well trained, such as they graduated from level five, they usually won't get up unless you motion them to. Don't let your dog sit there for too long that it becomes a bother for them.

Case Example: The Mailman and Alice

Alice is a young Miniature Schnauzer who loves to meet the mailman. Typically, this wouldn't be a problem, but Alice doesn't like the mailman to leave. She will try to bite his pants to get him to stay. Because Alice doesn't let go easily, she has started to ruin the mailman's uniform and he becomes a bit behind on his route. While he hasn't complained to Alice's owner, they don't want to cause any problems for the mailman. Therefore Alice's owner contacts a dog trainer they know.
The trainer told them to use Alice's best training skills to keep her from the mailman. "You don't want her to get too close, especially to his clothes. The first trick I would try is getting her to stay sitting when the mailman approaches. Also, keep the e-collar on for when she won't listen, but you need to be cautious about using the e-collar. You don't want her to become afraid of people, and this can happen if you send her the tone when she is heading to him. The best time to use the collar is when she doesn't listen to letting go of his clothing."

The next day, Alice and her owner waited for the mailman. The owner couldn't help but chuckle at her little furry friend because Alice stood so proud as she waited. Soon, she could notice him and became excited. "Sit" Alice's owner told her whenever she stood up. She would listen to the command, but once she became excited again, she would stand back up. By the time the mailman walked into the fenced yard, Alice couldn't contain her excitement anymore. She ran up to the mailman and followed him all the way to the house, which is their routine.

The problem doesn't begin until the mailman gets closer to the fence to leave. Right when Alice's owner noticed her dog about to go for his clothing, they snapped their fingers twice, catching Alice's attention. The owner then said "sit." Alice sat and looked at the mailman as he walked closer to the fence. Alice looked back to her owner, who didn't say or do anything. By the time Alice turned around, the mailman shut the fence door. He waved bye to Alice and carried on with his route.

Over the course of a couple weeks, Alice learned that she could follow the mailman to the house, but when he got close to the fence after dropping off the mail, she had to sit and allow him to leave. Because Alice is well-trained and her owners are consistent, the e-collar never had to be used for this situation.

Use "Come" When You Get a Chance

You don't need to be in a certain spot to tell your dog to "come." Once they are trained in this trick, you can use it when you want your dog to come to you. For example, if you want them to eat their evening meal, you will get their attention by calling their name and saying "come." The key is you need to listen to make sure they heard you. If they are playing in the next room with the kids, they might not hear you call them. Don't assume that you need to use the e-collar immediately. Take the remote and check to see if your dog can hear you call them. If you open the door to a lot of noise and they are playing, it's safe to assume they didn't hear you. Grab their attention and say "come." If they don't follow you because they are too distracted, then you will use the e-collar.

Take Your Dog for Car Rides

Most dogs love to ride in cars, so getting them into the car will not be a problem. If your dog is a little older, you may need to help them into the vehicle. Before you tell your dog to get into the car, you need to think of where you want your dog to stay. You also want to think of what you are going to do if you are driving and your dog gets in your way or a smaller dog tries to jump out of the window. Typically, these instances are rare and you can take precautions so they don't happen. For example, you will have your dog sit in the back seat until you know how they are going to react in the car. Another tip is not to leave your window low so that your dog can jump out.

Taking your dog on a car ride when you need to run an errand is a great way to practice "stay" with your dog. Of course, you need to make sure that your dog is safe and they won't get too hot in the car. Don't stay in the store long as your dog can become upset if they are not used to being alone in the car for an extended period of time. Remember to reward your dog with positive reinforcement when you return to the vehicle. If you have a larger dog, you can bring your dog out to play for a bit. They can stretch their legs or run around and catch a frisbee. It's always a great idea to bring toys with you just in case you have the opportunity to play with your dog.

There are a lot of drive thru places, such as banks, that will give your furry friend a treat and say hi. Even if it is through the window, your dog is interested in the new person and can't wait to get the treat they see!

Car rides are a great opportunity for your dog to learn more social skills. Other than the drive thru, you can take time to stop at a store that allows dogs and let them roam. You need to follow store policy, such as keeping them on a leash, but they will meet other people and possibly other dogs.

Case Example: Minnie and the Store

Minnie is a nine-month-old Poodle. Her companion, Paisley, adopted her from an animal shelter about two months ago. For help training Minnie, Paisley started taking her to obedience classes. Today, Minnie is in level three and struggling, so Paisley decided to take her dog out to a local pet store. She knows that Minnie suffers from a little social anxiety and wants her to become more at ease meeting new people and dogs. Paisley and Minnie's trainer talked about this situation, so Paisley feels prepared.

At first, everything went well. Paisley and Minnie walked up and down the dog isles where Minnie got to pick out a new toy. Paisley is now sitting on a bench where she is practicing "sit" and "stay" with Minnie when an energetic Golden Retriever comes walking up the aisle. At first, Minnie didn't seem too worried but showed interest in the dog. Minnie stood and started wagging her tail. Immediately, Paisley responded, "Minnie" to get her dog to look at her. Once she had Minnie's attention, Paisley told Minnie to "sit." Minnie obeyed, but still paid attention to the dog.

Looking at a dog book, Paisley's eyes scanned Minnie from time to time. She wasn't paying attention to the Golden Retriever until they became interested in Minnie. A young boy struggled to hold on to the leash of the Golden Retriever when the dog took off toward Minnie, causing the boy to let go. The boy started running and yelling at his dog, but Paisley remained calm. She got down to the level of the dogs and carefully watched Minnie and the other dog's reaction to each other. Both of them sniffed the other before they took a step back and looked at each other. Paisley become happy to notice that her dog hadn't moved, except for standing up.

Once the boy caught up to his dog, he grabbed the leash and apologized. Paisley told the little boy it is fine and talked about how the dogs are greeting each other. A few seconds later, the boy's mother came and the family left. Paisley looked at Minnie and praised her for being a good girl with the other dog.

A minute later, Minnie noticed another dog and started to show signs of distress. Paisley looked around and noticed a German Shepherd. This dog sat nicely by its owner and wasn't causing any trouble. Paisley started to care for her dog, trying to make Minnie feel better when the dog stood and started walking closer with its owner. Immediately, Minnie started barking and growling, causing the other dog to become defensive. Paisley started to practice the tricks that Minnie's trainer taught her, such as "no bark," but it didn't work. Minnie remained in defense mode.

Paisley started to feel a little panic, but remembered the trainer told her that Minnie will pick up on the panic, so Paisley remained calm. She then stepped in front of Minnie to create a block against the other dog. Once she noticed Minnie quiet down, Paisley turned around and said, "Minnie" and when her dog looked up, said, "walk" to motion Minnie to walk. Without a second thought about the other dog, Minnie turned and started walking toward the door.

The technique Paisley used with Minnie is known as "creating space" or "blocking the other dog." While this doesn't always work as some dogs will continue to look beyond their owner for the other dog, it worked for Minnie because they had trained for it in obedience school.

Aggressive Dogs

One of the most common problems dog owners have is meeting or noticing their dog becomes aggressive. It is important to note that your dog doesn't have to show signs of aggression prior to becoming aggressive. There are some situations, such as the above example with Minnie, when is it going to happen for various reasons. You may never understand why, but it is important to have a plan in place so you know how to handle these situations.

Paisley knew a bit about Minnie's history. She knew that Minnie lived with a larger dog that was mean to her at times. Therefore, Minnie would naturally become anxious or even aggressive when a larger dog approached her. So, before Paisley decided to take Minnie out to stores or around town where they could practice training in real life situations, she talked to Minnie's trainer, who helped Paisley come up with a few tricks to distract Minnie from larger dogs. Last on the list, was to send stimulation to Minnie through the e-collar. Because Minnie listened to Paisley when she said "go," Minnie did not receive the tone or shock.

Other than creating space, there are several other ways to handle aggressive dogs.

Keep Any Greetings Short

Some dogs don't mind running into another dog because they are curious animals. They want to smell the dog and say "hi," but then they want to continue on with their walk or don't care for the dog or the other owner. When this happens, your dog might become aggressive, just as Minnie did.

At the first sign you see of any type of aggressiveness, such as barking or growling, you need to take your dog out of the situation. One of the biggest mistakes people make is telling their dog "no" or to get angry. This is only going to cause the dog to become more aggressive because they feed off your emotions. At the same time, they might be warning you and they feel like you are ignoring this warning. It's always important to remember that dogs are protective. If they feel something isn't right they are going to take action. There comes a time when you need to listen to your dog and allow them to say "The conversation is over, let's move along."

In general, the best way to avoid any chances of this occurring is to keep greetings short. Even if you meet someone you know, if your dog is unfamiliar with the dog, person or seems uneasy, it is time to move on. Tell your friend you will give them a call and continue walking with your dog.

Another reason to keep greeting short is because your dog can become obsessed with the other dog. While this doesn't always pose a problem with aggression, it can for the other dog. If you do strike up a conversation, move your dog every few seconds and acknowledge them. This is also a good trick to follow if you meet a new dog and someone you don't know. Your dog can become stubborn and not want to continue on the walk because they want to say "hey" to the other dog. If it's okay with the other dog owner, let the dogs meet, but keep your dog moving at the same time. Slowly walk away from the dog and call your dog every few seconds to get their attention.

Notice How the Other Dog Is Acting

Even if you and your dog notice another dog approaching at the same time, you still have room to react to avoid a confrontation. Not only should you notice how your dog is reacting, but also the other dog. If you see any type of signs of aggressiveness from either dog, it's time to move your dog in another direction. You may have to do this by distracting your dog or creating a block from the other dog, so they decide to go across the street. Of course, the first method to try is simply walking your dog in another direction. Typically, dogs are very quick to follow their owners. If you do this before your dog becomes too interested in the other dog, you won't have a problem. One of the biggest keys to avoiding any aggressiveness is to stay one step ahead by noticing the signs. This is usually the best way to avoid any problems.

Avoid Other Dogs

Another way to handle meeting other dogs and dog owners is simply to avoid them. If you notice them, your dog is going to become more interested. If you don't pay attention to them, your dog is going to learn to just keep walking. While they might still look and try to get a sniff of the other dog, it is easier to tell them to come without much of a struggle.

Intermediate Level Tricks for Dogs

It is essential that all dogs receive basic training, discussed in the previous chapter. Now, I want to take training to another level and look at some of the tricks your dog can learn at the intermediate level. As long as your dog is healthy and interested in learning, they can perform these tricks. However, none of them are necessary. They are tricks that you can use as conversation starters or to surprise people. They are tricks that will allow your dog to show off.

Fetch

Teaching most dog breeds to fetch is pretty easy, it is almost like some of them have this trick in their body chemistry. But, there are other dogs that will struggle learning how to fetch. Not everyone feels the e-collar is necessary for fetching unless there is a possibility of your dog running away or causing trouble with people or other dogs.
There are three main skills your dog needs to know when it comes to learning how to play fetch:
1. Get it
2. Bring it
3. Drop it

Some people like to call the third skill "give it." The trouble with this is if your dog is playing with someone who isn't used to them, your dog could accidently bite the person's hand. For example, your nephews are visiting and want to play fetch with your dog. You agree and everyone heads outside. You've trained your dog to give you the ball, but you have to grab the ball out of their mouth for them to understand. You have never had a problem with your dog accidentally biting you or scratching with their teeth. Therefore, you aren't worried about anything happening to your nephews. In fact, you don't even think about the possibility.

As everyone is playing, you see your nephew hold on the ball in your dog's mouth. You notice your dog acting normal, but suddenly your nephew backs away and starts crying. You run to him, asking what is wrong. He shows you that one of your dog's teeth cut his finger.

You know this is an accident on your dog's part, so you don't discipline your dog. In fact, they look concerned about the situation. You take your nephew in, get the wound cleaned up well, and bandage it up. You know you have to watch it just in case there are signs of infection. You take a moment to think about how this can happen again as the neighborhood kids love to play fetch with your dog. It's at that moment you decide to teach your dog to "drop it" instead of "give it."

Talking to your dog's trainer, they tell you the best way to do this is by walking through the whole training process with them. Your trainer stated, "You don't want to just change part of the game without walking through the whole game. While your dog will have no trouble with the first two steps, you will need to take your time changing "give it" to "drop it."

One key tip for teaching your dog to play fetch is to have two toys that are exactly the same. You will play fetch with one while you hide the other one in your back pocket or somewhere out of their vision. You want them to focus on one toy at the time.

Step One: Tease Your Dog with the Toy

Whenever you want to play fetch with your dog, you need to get them interested in the toy. This is often caused "teasing." You can do this in many ways, as I am sure you have seen other people tease their dog before throwing a toy. You can talk to your dog to get them interested or act like you are throwing it in different directions before you really throw it.

Depending on your dog's age will depend on how excited they get for the toy and game. Older dogs might not be interested in playing fetch. However, younger dogs are going to love this game. If your dog isn't interested, try a different toy. If they are still not interested, they might be tired or want to do something else. Follow your dog's cues to notice if they are interested in something else. If a dog wants to play, they will let you know. If they are tired and want a break, they will inform you of this also.

Step Two: Toss the Toy

Once you get your dog's attention with the toy and they are ready to have it, toss it a few feet. Don't toss it very far at first as you still need to teach them the rest of the steps. When your dog picks up the toy and holds it in their mouth, praise them. You can run up to them and tell them what a good dog they are or use your regular praising method.

Step Three: Bring It

It is now time to teach your dog to bring the toy back to you. This can be one of the hardest parts because if a dog is not used to fetch, they will run off with the toy. Because of this, you want to make sure your dog understand where they can run off to and where they can't. If your dog goes beyond home base and you have their e-collar on, give them the tone to come back without saying or doing anything. They won't associate the tone or shock to their toy or play time, they will contribute it to going beyond their perimeter. Once they come back, praise them and continue to train them on bringing the toy back to you.

The easiest way to train your dog to bring the toy is to say your dog's name followed by "bring it." For example, "Princess, bring it" and when your dog takes two steps toward you, praise them. Go to them, grab the toy, and play a game of tug with them for a few seconds. This is when you gently try to take the toy out of your dog's mouth. The key is to let your dog win, meaning you let go of the toy while it is still in their mouth.

Step Four: Give It

At this point, you will give your dog the next cue to give the toy back to you. Take out the identical toy and tease them with it. This will get them to drop the toy in their mouth and focus on the toy in your hand.
Throw the toy a bit father this time, as you want to pick up the toy your dog dropped and place it behind you without them knowing you have it. Again, when your dog picks up the identical toy and walks toward you, praise them.

Step Five: Use the Word "Fetch"

You will repeat the first four steps by using the key words "get it," "bring it," and "drop it." After your dog has a handle on playing fetch, you will then start using the word "fetch."
When you throw the toy after teaching her, say "fetch, get it." Once your dog has the toy in their mouth, say "bring it," and when they bring it to you, say "drop it."
Once you start using the word fetch, you can slowly increase your distance. If you are at home, remember not to throw beyond your dog's perimeter. If they get distracted or go beyond their limits, use the e-collar to get them back into the perimeter.

Spin and Twist

When you teach a dog "spin and twist" you are teaching them 360 degree turns. This trick isn't typically taught to senior dogs as they don't have good balance. It is a great trick to teach puppies and some older dogs. Again, you know your dog the best. If you feel that this trick isn't for your dog, then you can skip to the next trick.
There are two main skills your dog will need to learn to accomplish this trick:
1. When your hand moves in the counterclockwise motion and you say "twist," they perform this action.
2. When your hand moves in a clockwise motion and you say "spin," they perform this action.

Step One: Halfway Spin

Start by having your dog stand or sit in front of you. With a treat between two fingers in your right hand, let the dog see the treat. Lure your dog in a clockwise half circle. Visually mark the point your dog reached and bring the treat back to you. Drop the treat by your right foot. This should get the dog to face you again. If they become distracted before or after the treat gain their attention. If this doesn't work, use the stimulation on their e-collar to gain their attention. Once they are calm and sitting or standing next to you again, move on to step two.

Step Two: Halfway Twist

Follow the directions from step one, but use your left hand instead of your right. Have your dog turn halfway counterclockwise and then drop the treat next to your left foot. Make sure you have their attention before moving on.

Step Three: Add the Verbal Cues

Once your dog has caught on to your luring, add in the verbal cues of "twist" when your dog moves counterclockwise or left, and "spin" for clockwise or right. Always remember to alternate between right and left.

Step Four: Start Phasing Out the Treats

Start with your right hand. Hold your hand up like you have a treat and continue to lure your dog half way. When your dog is looking at you, bring their attention to your left hand. Make sure they notice the treat so they don't become distracted by looking for the invisible treat. Once your dog makes the halfway turn, drop the treat.

Step Four: Complete the Circle

Keep using the treats in your left hand, but none in your right. Lure your dog through the whole way starting with a spin and then going for a twist. Remember to use your hand gestures and say the word as you are using the whole circle. Don't do this too much as your dog can become dizzy. Once they have follow command a few times, drop the treat and praise them.

Step Five: Add Speed and Mix Directions

Once your dog has a good handle on step four, you can start moving them a little faster and mixing up the direction. This means that you can have your dog twist twice, spin once, twist once, and then spin twice. At this point, you can keep the treat for when they are done spinning and twisting.

Chapter 7

Advanced Training with E-Collars

Now that you have the basic training and a couple of intermediate level tricks to teach your dog, let's focus on the more advanced training. When you get to this point with your e-collar, you will find that you don't need to use them too often. People will often send their dog the stimulation because they become distracted, aren't listening, or they leave their perimeter. But, because dogs are curious animals and easily distracted, it is always best to keep the e-collar on them when they are in the middle of training.

Will I Stop Training?

One of the biggest questions people ask if they will ever stop training their dog. My honest answer to this is it is really up to you. However, you should always practice the training your dog knows with them. While they will remember to "sit" when you tell them to, even if it's been a few days, if you become sloppy with training then they will follow this path. This means they will focus more on distractions than what you are saying. This will cause you to use the e-collar often. Plus, you will notice all the work you and your dog put into training is disappearing. So, while I do not advise that you stop training, it is always up to you.

Another reason you don't want to stop training is you can avoid having to reinforce any training. If you slack on training or stop telling them to sit, lay down, or stay they will start to ignore the commands. When this happens you will start to have trouble with your dog and become frustrated. You will tell them commands, but they will ignore you. This is when you need to reinforce all the training, starting with the basic tricks. To do this, you will want to start over.

Readjusting the E-Collar for a Growing Dog

Another factor to remember is to watch the e-collar. If your dog is growing, this means that collar has to grow with your dog. While you don't need to go through all the steps to get your dog adjusted to the e-collar, you will want to place the dummy collar on them when you need to clean the collar, charge it, or fix the strap so the e-collar will fit them correctly. Of course, if you don't always have the e-collar on your dog, you can do this when they are sleeping or taking a break.

Agility Training

To focus on agility training, you need a dog that is easy to train. Breeds that strive on obedience are the best dogs for this type of training. Dogs that are stubborn can learn agility training, but frustration can easily set in. Many people who have harder to train dogs give up when it comes to this type of training. It takes a lot of dedication and hard work from you and your dog, especially if they are a stubborn breed, but it is always worth it in the end.

Because of the in-depth process of agility training, I will not focus on how to teach your dog certain tricks. Most people will go to an obedience school to get the best agility training because of its advanced nature. Instead, I am going to give you tips to help you decide if agility training is right for your furry companion.

First, agility training is teaching your dog to run through obstacles. Dogs that perform on dog shows are taught in agility training. Some of the obstacles dogs usually learn are:

- The pause table
- Dog walk
- Tunnel
- Weave poles

Basic Training Before the E-Collar

Like with most training, the majority of people like to get past the basic training before they start using the e-collar. Instead, you will focus on a regular form of training you use, such as hand gestures, verbal cues, or a clicker. Clickers often work great because it is easy to gradually switch from a clicker to an e-collar.

Agility Training Is Great for Your Dog's Health

One of the biggest reasons people get their dogs into agility training is because it helps them stay healthy. Because they are so active, they burn off a lot of energy and they stay in shape. One of the most important factors is that you have to make sure your dog eats right or they will struggle when it comes to agility training.

There Are Risks

Unfortunately, agility training is a type of training that involves a lot of risks. Dogs need to pass a check-up by a veterinarian to make sure they are in good physical health for the tricks they will learn. This is an important part that you don't skip. For various reasons, dogs can have brittle bones and if they fall or trip over something while training, they could easily hurt themselves.

You also want to think about the heat. Your dog is going to run and stay highly active throughout their training, which tends to last longer than typical training. They are pushed by the trainers and will require more water, especially if it's hot outside. They will also need more breaks than normal if this is the case.

Using the E-Collar

When your dog becomes comfortable with the basic level of agility training, it's time to bring in the e-collar. Using the e-collar for agility training is different from other forms of training. For example, when you use the e-collar for home base training, you send the tone and shock to your dog when they leave their home base and don't come back when called. For agility training, you want them to keep running. You want them to run, jump, and follow the obstacles as much as possible. Instead of correcting your dog's behavior with the e-collar, you are redirecting their behavior.

When you redirect your dog, you are focusing on their agility route. They are following the rules and are running with you. For instance, Tammy's dog, Barnie, is learning his first agility route. As a puppy, Barnie is easily distracted and interested in almost anything he sees. Therefore, he tends to struggle following Tammy as she runs his route with him. When Tammy started using the e-collar, she decided should would call Barnie and ask him to "come." If he didn't listen, she would send him the signal from the e-collar. This immediately makes Barnie turn back to Tammy and they continue on his route. Within a week, Barnie is running the route beside Tammy without too much distraction. Within a couple of weeks, he is running the route by himself. Of course, Tammy still keeps a close eye on Barnie and will send him signals when he becomes distracted. Once Barnie reaches this point, Tammy and his trainer start adding new skills to his routine.

Adding New Skills

As the story about Barnie shows, you want to make sure your dog understands the basis of their route and know they need to keep going, ignoring distraction, before you add more skills. When you do get to the point of adding more, make sure that you only add one skill at the time. Once your dog incorporates this skill into their routine, then you can add another skill.

It is important that you continue to use the e-collar throughout this type of training. It is often known as the "silent enforcer" because you don't need to say anything. The second your dog goes off path, you send them the signals and watch them head back into their routine.

Roxie Jumped Over a Bar

Roxie's owner, Dustin, wanted to know if his dog would be good for agility training. After talking to Roxie's trainer, he received some tips and a guide to teach Roxie how to jump over a bar. The trainer stated if Roxie can accomplish this task, she is one step closer to agility training.
When it comes to agility competitions, dogs will jump as high as 24 inches. However a few have jumped higher. Dustin's goal isn't to get Roxie to jump high, so he decides to set the bar at its lowest setting, which is something the trainer advised him to do.

Step One: Walk Over the Bar

To get Roxie used to going over the bar, because all she wanted to do was go around it, Dustin got her leash and walked over the jump bar with her. At first, Roxie was a little hesitant to walk over the bar, but once she saw Dustin go over it, she followed.
Dustin repeated this action a couple of times and then started to say the word "over" each time they walked over the bar. Once they were over, Dustin gave Roxie positive reinforcement. Before he knew it, Roxie was interested in going over the bar again, specifically for the positive reinforcement.

Step Two: Roxie Walks Over the Bar Alone

Next, Dustin set Roxie in front of the bar and told her to "sit" and "stay." He then placed the bar on the next highest setting and said, "Roxie, come." The minute Roxie started to go over the bar, Dustin said "over." Dustin would repeat this action a couple of times before moving the bar up a notch.

Step Three: Roxie Jumps Over the Bar

Getting Roxie to jump over the bar wasn't the easiest part of the training, but Dustin understood this. Once the bar got to Roxie's elbow, she decided to dive underneath the bar. Dustin rewarded Roxie for her efforts and had her try again. This time, Dustin said "over" right as Roxie got to the bar. Roxie stopped, looked at the bar, and tried to jump over. Unfortunately, she knocked the bar down. Again, Dustin rewarded Roxie for her efforts.

It is at this point that Dustin starts to incorporate the e-collar. Instead of giving a visual cue, Dustin is going to say the word "over" when Roxie is supposed to jump. While she might not make it every time, if she refuses to jump, Dustin is going to give her a signal. Dustin's goal is to eventually stop saying the word "over" and simply give a signal to get Roxie to jump on time.

Step Four: Using the E-Collar

Dustin decided to help Roxie a little more by getting down to her level. Standing on his knees near the bar, he told Roxie to "come." Once she got to the bar, he told Roxie "over" and gave a signal. Roxie walked up to the bar, but simply looked at Dustin. He then repeated the signal. Right as Roxie jumped up, Dustin said "over" and gave another signal. He found Roxie on the other side. She had finally jumped over the bar without tripping or knocking it over. Dustin rewarded Roxie, and they continued this process a few more times without lifting the bar.

Boing

If you want to train your dog to jump over the bar but notice they struggle with their jump, then you can try a trick known as boing, which is when your dog jumps in the air on cue. When people use the e-collar for this type of training, they will usually switch to the e-collar instead of using a verbal cue. However, it is recommended that you start the training by using the verbal cue of "jump" or "boing" and not the e-collar.

Step One: Lure Your Dog to Jump

To lure your dog to jump, it's best to have a treat in your hand. You will crouch down a little and then spring up onto your toes. When you jump, you want to make sure that your arm is up as this is more likely to make your dog jump up because they want the treat.

Step Two: Use Verbal Cues

Once your dog starts to jump with you, add in the verbal cue "boing." Continue to jump as you were until you feel that your dog can jump up to your verbal cue.

Step Three: Use the E-Collar

When you start using the e-collar, you will still want to use the verbal cue as you send your dog a signal. Once you have repeated this action a few times, you can start to get your dog to jump higher. You will continue to use treats to accomplish this mission. For instance, you can first hold the treat between your fingers and raise your hand to where you want your dog to jump. Once they get high enough, you can hold the treat in the palm of your hand. By this point, you should have to use any verbal cues. Instead, you will focus on the e-collar's signal.

Hunting

Similar to agility training, you are going to use the e-collar for hunting once your dog understands the basics. It is also meant to redirect their behavior and not correct it. One of the basic tips for hunting with an e-collar is to get one specifically designed for hunting. While they are more expensive, you can reach your dog up to one mile, which is great when you want to call your dog back to you.

Teach Your Dog the Route

Before you take your dog out hunting, make sure that you planned out a route. You can start by taking your dog on a walk, preferably with a leash unless they are great at staying by your side and not running off. While you can use the e-collar, because you are training them for hunting, most people like to use the e-collar later in their training.
You want your dog to become used to the route. Take your time and let them smell and mark their territory. Don't hurry them along the route because they can easily forget it. You should take your dog on the route a few times before going onto the next step.

Make Sure to Train Your Dog to Return Home

Taking your dog hunting can be a scary time for a dog owner, especially at first. There is always a possibility your dog can get a bit lost–or you lost from your dog as they have a great smelling nose to find their way back to you or their home. However, you should always make sure that your dog understands how to return home. Before you start this process in your hunting training, you will want to make sure you and your dog understand home base training.
Another tip when it comes to training your dog to return home is to have a special signal. For example, you might give them two signals if you want them to return home instead of one.

Repetition Is Key

Like with all other types of training, repetition is key when it comes to hunting training. You always want to make sure you take time to show your dog what they need to do on their hunting adventure. Many owners will spend time every year retraining their dog for hunting, especially if they only go deer or duck hunting. This type of repetition is mainly for safety and to ensure your dog remembers what they are supposed to do.

Chapter 8

Common Mistakes

By now you understand that the e-collar is one of the biggest training tools for dogs. While there is controversy, if you use the e-collar correctly, your dog will thrive. Unfortunately, no matter how much you learn about e-collar training, mistakes can happen.

Lack of Consistency in Training

One of the most common mistakes is a lack of consistency in training. Because I have talked about consistency through this book, I won't spend too much time on it here. However, it is important to discuss as a mistake.

No matter where you are, if your dog does something that they aren't supposed to, you need to inform them of this correctly and immediately. Dogs are not going to understand what they did wrong 15 minutes ago. They live in the moment and need to be corrected right away. If you wait a few minutes, you are going to confuse your dog and they will associate the shock to whatever they were doing at the time. This can cause a lot of issues if you're not careful.

Training Your Dog for Too Long

It is important that you limit the amount of time you train your dog, especially in one setting. Younger dogs shouldn't be trained in one setting for more than five minutes while older dogs can generally last about ten minutes. If you struggle with time, you can set a timer on your phone. This will alert you to when it is time to give your dog a break.

When you don't pay attention to the time, you can overwork your dog. This can cause them to become stressed, tired, and sick over time. Plus, if it is hot you need to make sure that your dog gets plenty of breaks to cool down and water. They will need more water than normal if they are training outside on a hot day.

Dog Owners Don't Send a Signal Immediately

One of the most common mistakes happens when the transmitter isn't close to you and your dog misbehaves. For instance, you are in the kitchen when you notice your dog in the living room chewing on the couch cushion. You quickly scan the room for your remote and notice it is on the table in the living room. As you walk into the living room to grab it, your dog turns their attention onto a chew toy on the floor. Once you grab the remote, you push the button to give your dog a warning and shock. Unfortunately, your dog is no longer chewing on the cushion, so they associate the shock to their own toy. If you don't keep your remote with you at all times, there will be moments you don't get to train your dog when they take part in unwanted behavior. This is something you want to avoid doing. Even if you are in your home, have the remote clipped to your pants or in your pocket so you can quickly grab it when you need to. This will not only make sure you can catch your dog when you need to, but will make training more consistent.

You Wait Too Long to Start Training

It is sometimes hard to know when the perfect time to start training is. There are general rules of thumb, but this doesn't mean it's right for every dog. One key is you want to start training your dog as soon as you bring them home. Even if they are potty trained and only eight weeks old, you need to make sure they start learning home base, where to sleep, where to eat, and the rules of the house right away. Many people don't think of these factors as training, but they are. Whenever you are teaching your dog something new, it is a form of training.

People Become Codependent on the E-Collar

The key to using the e-collar as a training tool is to get your dog to stop the unwanted behavior. Once the behavior as ceased, you need to wean your dog from the e-collar. If you continue to use the e-collar or you use it for all forms of training, you will find yourself become dependent on the e-collar. When this happens, your dog is also going to become dependent on the e-collar. Dogs who are dependent on the e-collar need to feel the warning vibration, tone, or shock to know they are doing something they shouldn't. If they don't feel one of these, they will continue to take part of that behavior.

You Don't Give Your Dog Enough Training Time

When you start training, you need to understand that you will train your dog often and you won't stop. Even when your dog has learned the basics, you will continue to train them. One of the biggest mistakes people make is they train their dogs the basic commands, when they want them to sit, lay down or get down, and then don't focus on any actual training time. This doesn't give your dog enough time to really learn the foundations of training.

Always spend time every day training your dog. Enroll them in an obedience class and get to know a professional dog trainer for extra help in case you ever need it.

The Dog Has Not Received Any Type of Prior Training

The e-collar is not meant to start training your dog the basics. It is meant to help your dog understand that certain issues are not appropriate, after they have received other types of training. For example, you will not use the e-collar on your dog when you are potty training them. First, most dogs are potty trained within a couple months of age, meaning they are too young for the e-collar. Second, using the e-collar when you catch your dog going to the bathroom can cause them to feel like that behavior is wrong. They won't associate the shock to the fact they didn't use the right are to go; they will associate it with their actions. This can make dogs feel that they are doing something wrong whenever they need to go potty.

Most people who use the e-collar right away, meaning without any prior training, are people who believe the e-collar is used as punishment or they don't understand the e-collar. You should never believe that the e-collar should be used as a form of punishment. Most e-collar companies advise against this and all dog trainers do.

You Use Harsh Discipline

It's a given that you will need to discipline your dog from time to time. For example, you might send them into a special kennel for a "time out" when they scratch the wall. However, most trainers state the best ways dogs learn is through training and positive reinforcement. While you may not completely believe this, you should never use any type of harsh discipline, such as hitting, staring down, grabbing them by the neck, jerking their leash, or yelling. Using this type of discipline can cause your dog to become aggressive and fearful. You can also harm your dog through some of these actions.
If you need help in understanding how to gain better control over your dog's behavior, the best place to go is obedience school. They will help you learn the ropes of training and make sure that your dog understands what behaviors are acceptable and which ones aren't.

People Don't Understand How the E-Collar Works

One of the most common mistakes people follow is getting the e-collar and immediately putting it on their dog and using it. Sometimes people will try it out, even if the dog isn't taking part in unwanted behavior, to see how their dog reacts. This is a huge mistake and something you should never do. You must allow your dog to get use to the e-collar before you use it. Furthermore, you have to wait until they are doing something you want to change before you give them a warning and then shock. If you are going to use the e-collar to train your dog, always use it correctly.

Chapter 9

Frequently Asked Questions and Answers

There are many common questions people ask about training their dog. Trainers find this part of their job enjoyable because they want to help people and dogs have the best training experience possible.

Question #1: Do Different Breeds of Dogs Learn Differently?

A lot of people wonder if they have a certain breed of dog, if they need to train them in a certain way. The straight answer to this question is no. All dogs, no matter what breed or age, learn the same. They can learn the same tricks with the same steps, tips, and strategies. As long as you are consistent and follow the steps within this guide, you can train any breed with an e-collar successfully.

Questions #2: Do I Wean My Dog Off the E-Collar?

Yes, you shouldn't continue to depend on the e-collar if you don't need to. If you feel your dog is successfully trained in the task, slowly wean them off the e-collar. You can do this by placing a dummy e-collar on your dog when you would have given them the e-collar. Remember, your dog shouldn't realize that the e-collar is what gave him the shocks. They should believe it was their behavior. As long as you trained your dog successfully with an e-collar, weaning is a breeze.

You can place the e-collar aside until you need to train your dog again or you find yourself bringing home another new family members. Remember, when you are not going to use the e-collar for a period of time, you want to make sure it won't go off randomly, meaning turn your e-collar off and put it away.

Question #3: How Do I Know the E-Collar Isn't Harming My Dog?

The only way you will know is by watching and understanding your dog's reactions to the e-collar. If they whine, become frightened, cry, or show any signs of distress when you shock your dog, the stimulation levels are too high. Simply lower the level to the lowest setting and adjust as you need to. The dog should only slightly move its head when it feels the shock.

Most dogs respond to the lowest level of stimulation. While this does give them a little discomfort, it does not hurt them. Most trainers will tell you that a little discomfort is fine when it comes to keeping your dog safe and healthy.

At the same time, most trainers will tell you if you are afraid to use the e-collar, you shouldn't use it. As stated before, try the e-collar on yourself before you place it on the dog. This might ease your mind about how it will hurt your dog.

Question #4: How Do I Know When to Start Using the E-collar?

The simple answer is when you feel the time is right. Most people say that dogs should be at least six months old before they receive the e-collar because of the weight and size of the collar. The key is to do your research and make sure that you spend enough time going over your preparations for e-collar training. For example, you know your house rules, you know how you want to train your dog, and you are looking for a dog trainer to help you with the process.
Of course, you don't need to have a professional dog trainer on your side. However, it is always a great idea to get your furry friend enrolled in a training class for extra support and social time.

Question #5: I Have Seen Other Dogs React Negatively to the Shock from the E-Collar. How Do I Know My Dog Won't?

This is a great question. The truth is, a dog can react negatively to the e-collar for many reasons. First, they are not trained properly with the e-collar. For instance, the stimulation level may be too high or they receive a shock for every little thing they do wrong. You should never use the e-collar in this way. You only want to use the e-collar for certain training procedures.

Second, the dog may be more sensitive than other dogs. Just like humans, each dog has their own personality and there are several dogs that are highly sensitive. This will cause a dog to feel the shocks strongly, stronger than other dogs. This will also cause them to internalize the shock more than other dogs, causing them to become sad or even depressed. In general, if you have a highly sensitive dog, you might not need to use the e-collar. Highly sensitive dogs tend to follow instructions through a person's tone of voice a lot better than anything else.

Conclusion

If your head seems like it is overloaded with information, this is typical when it comes to dog training, especially if you are beginning this journey. Fortunately, this book is here for you whenever you need it as you can simply download the book and have it in your phone or on your device for whenever you need it.

Even if you feel you might need to reread some information before you start training your dog, especially when it comes to the training steps, I know you have a better idea about e-collar training and how you can incorporate the e-collar into various tricks.

One great fact about this book is it not only explains what e-collar training is, but you also receive a number of tricks to teach your dog. This book didn't simply focus on the basics, it also looked at more advanced training techniques.

Some of the most important takeaways from this book are:

- Making sure you dog becomes used to the e-collar before you bring it into training. You never want to put the collar on and start giving your dog signals. This is going to cause your dog stress as they will be confused about what is going on. Furthermore, they will know that you are doing this to them and the trust between you and your dog will start to fade.

- You have to be consistent as a dog trainer. It doesn't matter if you are in your home or at a friend's house, when your dog does something they shouldn't, you need to be quick and correct their behavior. Remember, dogs only focus on what is going on at the moment. If you give them signals from the e-collar a few seconds after the unwanted behavior, the dog is going to associate the signals to what they are doing at that moment. Always notice what your dog is doing when you are in the middle of training, and be ready to act to help them learn that some behavior is not acceptable.

- E-collars will not harm your dog unless you have the collar on too tight or the stimulation level too high. Always make sure you can fit two fingers between your dog's neck and the collar. Start the stimulation level at the lowest setting and wait until you need to use it on your dog to correct their behavior. If they turn their head or react in a slight way, they noticed the stimulation. If they didn't respond at all, it is time to adjust the level. Remember to only move the stimulation level up one. If your dog whines or whimpers when you give a signal, the level is too high and you need to bring it back down.

- Make sure that you don't buy the wrong collar for your dog. Some e-collars are not meant for small dogs. Dogs that are under a few months old shouldn't be given an e-collar. While most people feel the general rule is about six months old, you can start your dog on the e-collar earlier. It really depends on the amount of training they have. It is important to note that there are tons of great e-collars available to you. There are so many that I couldn't include them all in this book. Do your research to make sure you really do pick the best e-collar for your dog.

- Always find a way to gain your dog's attention before you start training them. Even if you've trained your dog for two years, you always want to grab their attention. Dogs are naturally easily distracted, and it isn't fair to them to send them signals when you didn't let them know that you wanted them to follow your command. Use their name or find another method, such as snapping your fingers twice, to gain their attention.

- Always reward your dog with positive reinforcement when they are training. Even if they make a mistake, you want to reward their efforts. You don't always need to give them a treat. Taking time to play with them and talking to them is a great way to give your dog positive reinforcement.

- While dogs can receive training at any age, you always want to keep your dog's age in mind because at the end of the day, it does matter. Puppies are going to be more energetic, which can make you feel more frustrated with training. Older dogs are going to be slower, which means you need more patience. Another factor about older dogs is while they can train for longer periods of time, they will tire out sooner. Never push your dog to finish training or train longer when they are showing your signs that they are tired.

- Start training your dog as soon as you bring them home. Even if they are only 10 weeks old and are potty trained, you want to focus on the basics, such as where they eat, sleep, and their home base.

- Do whatever you can to make sure your dog eats healthy and gets enough sleep, as much as you can do this for a dog. Eating healthy and getting enough sleep will help ensure that you and your dog have the best training experience possible. Furthermore, this is something to do with your pets whether you train them or not. It is up to us to make sure they get food with the nutrients they need so they can live a long and healthy life.

- Don't become codependent on the e-collar. While you will use it often, most people believe the point of the e-collar is to correct your dog's behavior and then wean them off. If you become too dependent on the e-collar, then your dog will only react when they receive the stimulation. You want your dog to react to your commands and not the stimulation of the e-collar. Always remember the e-collar is more of a reinforcer when it comes to training.

- Dog training takes a lot of patience. You will need to repeat the steps over and over to give your dog the best training experience. Always remember that the number one factor with training is the safety and health of your dog. Once you keep this in mind, you can give yourself a breather when you start to feel frustrated or losing patience. You are trying to help your dog and not harm them in any way. Rushing through training is going to harm them mentally and emotionally. Furthermore, if you have the e-collar on too high and find yourself giving them signals often, you could end up physically hurting them.

- Follow the directions on how to put on the e-collar to ensure it is in the right location. If you place the e-collar on the base of your dog's neck, it will move up the neck when your dog is playing, This can cause them problems and they won't feel the signals.
- Enroll your dog in an obedience class. This will not only help your dog when it comes to training, but it will help you as well. You will meet a great dog trainer who can help you through some of the toughest times and meet like-minded individuals. Everyone you come in contact with in obedience class will become a part of your journey. Furthermore, your dog will get some social time, which is important. If you only have one dog, your dog can become lonely and feel isolated if you don't allow them to play with other dogs and meet other people. Obedience training is one of the best ways to do this.

Above all, you need to enjoy your time with your dog. Do what you can to make dog training fun. Of course, it will be more work that you can imagine. However, as you work with your dog and listen to them, they will listen to you. If you take the advice given to you about how to train your dog in basic commands as well as more advanced command, you can watch your dog thrive with everything he learns. Through the tips given to you in this book and remembering the key takeaway notes, you will have the best training journey possible with your furry companion. This will give them some of the best memories throughout their life. You will have a great relationship and your dog will spend many years as one happy, obedient, and loving dog.

References

5 Tips for Dog Training Session Prep. (2017). Retrieved 1 October 2019, from https://acmecanine.com/5-tips-dog-training-session-prep/

Accessories & Replacement Parts | E-Collar Technologies. Retrieved 28 September 2019, from https://www.educatorcollars.com/accessories

APDT - "Real Life" Training. Retrieved 2 October 2019, from http://www.trainyourdogmonth.com/tips/reallife.aspx

Arterburn, J., & Benson, K. Dog Shock Collar Myths and Misconceptions. Retrieved 21 September 2019, from https://www.securepets.com/debunkingmyths.html

Barkless Dog Collar | Barkless Pro Anit Bark Collar - E-Collar Technologies. Retrieved 26 September 2019, from https://www.ecollar.com/products/barkless-pro-anti-bark-collar

Bender, A. (2019). Our Top 10 Puppy Training Tips. Retrieved 29 September 2019, from https://www.thesprucepets.com/top-puppy-training-tips-1118511

Bennett, J. 7 Must-Read Tips When Buying a Purebred Dog. Retrieved 26 September 2019, from https://www.rover.com/blog/purebred-dog-tips/

Choosing a Puppy. (2019). Retrieved 17 September 2019, from http://www.apdt.co.uk/dog-owners/choosing-a-puppy

dog agility training for beginners: how to get started - SitStay. Retrieved 2 October 2019, from https://sitstay.com/blogs/good-dog-blog/dog-agility-training-for-beginners

E-Collar for Dogs - Remote Training Collars | E-Collar Technologies. Retrieved 27 September 2019, from https://www.ecollar.com/categories/remote-dog-trainers

Evans, B. (2018). Benefits of using Dog Training Collars that you can't ignore. Retrieved 27 September 2019, from https://petspy.com/blogs/dog-training/benefits-of-using-the-e-collar-training-that-you-can-t-ignore

Finlay, K. 5 Reasons You & Your Dog Should Take An Obedience Class. Retrieved 29 September 2019, from https://iheartdogs.com/5-reasons-you-your-dog-should-take-an-obedience-class/

How to Care for a Formerly Abused Pet. (2016). Retrieved 29 September 2019, from https://www.tasteofthewildpetfood.com/training-behavior/how-to-care-for-a-formerly-abused-pet/

Howell, A. (2019). The E-Collar Dog Training Bible : The All-Inclusive Guide, Including Specific E Collar Training For Golden Retrievers, German Shepherds, Labrador Retrievers, And Beagles. Kindle Edition.

Hunting Dog Collars | E-Collars for Hunting Dogs - E-Collar Technologies. Retrieved 26 September 2019, from https://www.ecollar.com/categories/hunting-dog-trainer

Krohn, L. (2017). Everything you need to know about E Collar Training. Retrieved 2 October 2019, from

Obedience Courses. Retrieved 2 October 2019, from https://www.animalhumanesociety.org/behavior/obedience-courses

Pavia, A. (2017). Adopting A Shelter Dog: 5 Tips For Success. Retrieved 23 September 2019, from https://fearfreehappyhomes.com/adopting-shelter-dog-5-tips-success/

Puppy Training and Socialization Tips for Owners. (2011). Retrieved 29 September 2019, from https://healthypets.mercola.com/sites/healthypets/archive/2011/09/22/every-puppy-owner-must-know-about-early-training-socialization.aspx

Ray. (2010). History of the Shock Collar. Retrieved 28 September 2019, from http://dogtrainingclub01.blogspot.com/2010/12/history-of-shock-collar_20.html

shibashake. Dog to Dog Aggression – Why and How to Stop It. Retrieved 2 October 2019, from https://shibashake.com/dog/dog-to-dog-aggression

Stregowski, J. (2019). Are You Guilty of These Dog Training Mistakes?. Retrieved 2 October 2019, from https://www.thesprucepets.com/common-dog-training-mistakes-4030442

Things to Consider When Choosing a Dog. (2017). Retrieved 17 September 2019, from https://trupanion.com/blog/2017/03/choosing-dog/

Train your dog: The relevance of consistency! | Tractive. (2018). Retrieved 28 September 2019, from https://tractive.com/blog/en/training-en/consistency-and-rituals-in-dog-training

Transitioning for Canines. Retrieved 29 September 2019, from https://primalpetfoods.com/pages/transitioning-for-canines

Where to get a puppy. Retrieved 28 September 2019, from https://www.humanesociety.org/resources/where-get-puppy

Wildesen, A. The Misunderstood Doberman Pinscher. Retrieved 17 September 2019, from https://thecaninetrainingcenter.com/the-misunderstood-doberman-pinscher/

Wilson, S. (2019). 8 Things You Need To Know Before Buying A Shock Collar | CanineJournal.com. Retrieved 27 September 2019, from https://www.caninejournal.com/shock-collar-for-dogs/